SIMON HOROBIN

bagels bumf & buses

A day in the life of the English language

OXFORD
UNIVERSITY PRESS

OXFORD
UNIVERSITY PRESS

Great Clarendon Street, Oxford, OX2 6DP,
United Kingdom

Oxford University Press is a department of the University of Oxford.
It furthers the University's objective of excellence in research, scholarship,
and education by publishing worldwide. Oxford is a registered trade mark of
Oxford University Press in the UK and in certain other countries

First Edition published in 2019

Impression: 1

Published in the United States of America by Oxford University Press
198 Madison Avenue, New York, NY 10016, United States of America

British Library Cataloguing in Publication Data

Data available

Library of Congress Control Number: 2019936810

ISBN 978-0-19-883227-0

Printed and bound in Great Britain by
Clays Ltd, Elcograf S.p.A.

This book is for Lucy, Rachel, and Florence, who quickly learned to preface every question about words with—'the short answer, please'. This is the long answer.

Contents

Preface

There are many books that investigate the origins of English words and phrases; but these tend to focus on unusual idioms and sayings—who was the real McCoy? why was Larry so happy? how did a cat come to die of curiosity? This book differs in focusing on the words and phrases we use every day—often without any thought as to their origins—examining where they came from, charting how their uses have evolved over the centuries, and temporarily reviving others that have fallen out of use. In short, this book is a celebration of the richness of the English language, and the fascinating stories that lie behind its word hoard.

The study of word origins is known as *etymology*, which is from a Greek root meaning 'true', reflecting the way that the ancient Greeks believed that the earliest form of a word revealed its authentic meaning. There are still those who insist that the correct meaning of English words may be determined by reference to their origins, and who claim (for instance) that *decimate* can only mean 'reduce by a tenth', since it is from Latin *decimus* 'tenth'. But if we were to follow such an approach, *December* should be the tenth month, as it was in the Roman calendar before January and February were added. And if we did insist on only sanctioning the use of *decimate* in its original sense—put to death one in every ten of an army of mutinous soldiers—how often would we use it?

Much more interesting than trying to restrict and dictate usage is the question of how and why the meanings of these words have come to change, and what they can tell us about the people who used them. That is the subject of this book.

PART I

Starting the Day

CHAPTER 1

Getting up

The alarm sounds and rouses you from a deep sleep. While we may consider the electronic buzzing of an alarm clock to be a pretty grim start to the day, the original use of *alarm* signalled a significantly more stressful situation. The word originates in the Italian *all'arme* 'to arms'—a distress call issued to alert an army to an oncoming attack. The word *alert* has a similar military origin, deriving from the Italian phrase *all'erta* 'on the watchtower'. Drawing back the curtains and looking out the window reveals that a new day has dawned. The word *dawn* is first recorded in the sixteenth century; before that the terms used were *dawning* or *dawing*. All three derive from the verb *to daw* (from Old English *dagian*), meaning 'to become day'. If this seems a rather unimaginative way to describe Homer's rosy-fingered or bright-throned dawn, don't blame the Anglo-Saxons, since they had a selection of more poetic alternatives.

The Dawn

The Anglo-Saxons were evidently early risers, since they coined a variety of words to describe first light. They even had a word for the hour before dawn—*uhtan*—that the rest of us would call the middle of the night. This was the hour when medieval monks celebrated the office of *uht-song*, now known by its Latin name *Matins* (still seen in the French for morning, *matin*). Old English also had a term for the sorrow and anxiety experienced at this time of the day, *uhtceare*, presumably coined by sleepy monks faced with the prospect of getting out of bed in a freezing cold dormitory (Latin *dormitorium* 'sleeping place') for *uht-song*. Another useful word for capturing that nebulous (Latin *nebulosus* 'cloudy') sense of foreboding that hangs over you first thing in the morning is *matu-tolypea*, a classical word literally meaning 'grief of the dawn'.

Other Anglo-Saxon words for dawn are compounds—a common way of forming new words in Old English (and all Germanic languages). *Day-rim*, literally 'border of the day', refers to dawn as the beginning of a new day. *Day-row*, whose second element means 'ray', figures the dawn as the bringer of light; this image lies behind other terms such as *rodor-lihtung* 'illumination of the heavens' and *day-red*—describing the colour of the sky. The later Middle Ages added some nicely uplifting words, such as *springing* and *uprising*. The fifteenth century also saw the adoption into English of the name of Aurora, the Roman goddess of the dawn, as well as the word *orient*. *Orient* is used today to refer to the countries of the East; the word originates in Latin *oriri* 'to rise', and so referred to the East as the land of the rising sun. The *occident*, the equivalent term for the West, has its origins in the Latin *occidere* 'to go down'—land of the setting sun. The image of the rising sun as an opening eye lies behind the sixteenth-century terms *peeping* and *peep of the day*. A more dramatic image in which the sun breaks through—which survives in modern English *daybreak* and *crack of dawn*—is found in *breach of the day*, *sun-break*, *prick of the day*, and *creek* (from a Dutch verb meaning 'burst through'). By contrast with these poetic terms and the images they conjure up, the nineteenth-century dialect *sparrow-farts*—'Tha mun be up by sparrowfarts or tha'll be too late'—seems rather crude.

Having established that there is no excuse to linger in bed any longer, it is time to consult the *calendar* (from Latin *Kalendae*, the term for the first day of the Roman month), before throwing back the covers and preparing for the day ahead.

The Days of the Week

The names we give to the days of the week go back to Old English, and were formed by simply translating the Latin equivalents. The Romans labelled the days of the week after the planets, which in turn were named after the Roman gods and goddesses. In most cases, the Roman names have continued in use in the modern *Romance* languages (languages derived from Latin, the language of Rome); compare, for instance, Latin *dies Lunae*, *dies Martis*, *dies Mercurii*, *dies Jovis*, *dies Veneris* with French *lundi*, *mardi*, *mercredi*, *jeudi*, and *vendredi*. In rendering these into English, the Anglo-Saxons replaced the Roman deities with equivalents from the Germanic *pantheon* (Greek *pan* 'all' and *theos* 'god'). So in *Tuesday*, *Wednesday*, *Thursday*, and *Friday* we see the replacement of the Roman gods Mars, Mercury, Jove, Venus, with the Germanic gods Tiw, Woden (the Anglo-Saxon equivalent of the Norse god Odin), Thunor (the Anglo-Saxon version of Norse Thor), and Frig (Odin's wife). The Roman days named after the sun and the moon, *dies Solis* and *dies Lunae*, were also translated into Old English, giving us *Sunday* and *Monday*. A similar pattern of replacements can be seen in other Germanic languages, such as German; compare German *Montag* 'Monday', *Donnerstag* 'Thursday' (literally 'Thunder Day'), and *Freitag* 'Friday'. *Dienstag* 'Tuesday' appears to show the replacement of the Roman god Mars with an alternative Germanic deity; the same origin lies behind Dutch *Dinsdag*. An alternative theory suggests that the first element is a term for a public assembly or council. But instead of naming *Wednesday* after the Germanic god *Woden*, modern German has adopted the more prosaic alternative *Mittwoch* 'mid-week'. This may originate in a translation of the Latin name *media hebdomas* 'middle of the week', used after the spread of Christianity throughout the Roman empire in preference to a term referring to a pagan deity.

Saturday is the odd one out, since here the Roman deity was preserved in English; thus Latin *dies Saturni* (day of Saturn) became Old English *Sæternesdæg*. But where English preserves the Latin name, the modern Romance languages have departed from that source: compare French *samedi*, Italian *sabato*, Spanish *sábado*. These names are instead taken from an alternative Latin term, *dies Sabbati* 'day of the Sabbath', which was adopted with the spread of the Christian religion. This Latin form was also taken up in German, hence modern German *Samstag*, whose first element originates in the Latin *sabbata*. An alternative German name, *Sonnabend* 'Sunday Eve', was formed using the Christian concept of the *vigil*—the eve of a holy day—as an occasion for religious observance (from Latin *vigil* 'awake, alert'—the origin of *vigilant*). Old English had an equivalent in *Sunnanæfen*, although this has not survived into modern English. Where English has preserved the earlier Roman name for Sunday, *dies solis*, the modern Romance languages derive their names from the later *dies Dominica* 'our Lord's day': French *dimanche*, Italian *domenica*, and Spanish *domingo*.

SAT

CHAPTER 2

Breakfasting

For many of us the day begins with a cup of tea; this drink was first imported into Britain early in the seventeenth century, becoming very popular by the 1650s. The London diarist Samuel Pepys drained his first cup in 1660, as recorded in his famous diary: 'I did send for a cup of tee (a China drink) of which I had never drunk before.' A love of tea is so ingrained in British life that the phrase *cup of tea* has come to stand for anything viewed positively. In the 1930s what interested someone was termed *their tea*; today we can express our dislike for something by saying: *it's not my cup of tea*. When someone is distressed or bereaved, we console them with *tea and sympathy*, a phrase taken from the title of a 1950s film. More recently, *tea* has seen a rise in use as a slang term for 'gossip', with those on social media imploring each other to *spill the tea*.

Tea

The word *tea* derives ultimately from the Mandarin Chinese word *chá*, via ('by way of', from Latin *via* 'road') the Min dialect form *te*. The Mandarin word is also the origin of the informal word *char*, heard today in phrases like *a nice cup of char*. The Chinese origin of the plant is remembered in the idiom *not for all the tea in China*, meaning 'certainly not', 'not at any price', which originated in Australian slang of the 1890s.

By the eighteenth century tea had become a symbol of fashionable society and a staple of the coffee house culture. Samuel Johnson was a self-confessed 'hardened and shameless tea-drinker...whose kettle has scarcely time to cool; who with tea amuses the evening, with tea solaces the midnight, and, with tea, welcomes the morning'. As tea-drinking developed into an elaborate social ritual, so did the associated paraphernalia. From the eighteenth century we find references to *tea-spoons, tea-boxes, tea-tongs, tea-kitchens* (similar to a modern *tea-urn*), *tea-caddies* (from *catty*, a unit of weight, ultimately derived from Malay *kati*); sets comprising cups, saucers, tea-pots, and other essentials were known as *tea-equipage*, or rather more prosaically as *tea-things*, or *tea-services* (as they still are today). The trade in growing, selling, and administering tea created a need for *tea-growers, tea-sifters*, and *tea-ladies* (nowadays associated with a *tea-trolley* and *tea-urn*); the grandest ceremonies were overseen by a *tea-hostess* or *tea-master* to ensure proper etiquette was observed.

The large sums of money involved in the importing of this luxury commodity prompted efforts to regulate the trade, resulting in *tea-tax, tea-duty*, and *tea-broker*. The Boston Tea Party of 1773, when British tea was offloaded from ships into Boston harbour in protest at taxation, is the inspiration behind the name of the US Republican Tea Party movement, although some commentators have interpreted this as a backronym (an unhistorical explanation of a word's origin, blending *back* and *acronym*) for 'taxed enough already'. Historical terms like *tea-user* and *tea-dealer* recall the lexicon of today's illicit drug trade, while in modern US slang a *tea-head* refers to someone who regularly smokes marijuana, and a *tea-pad* to a drugs den.

The drinking of tea became such an established feature of English social life that we find references to *tea-breakfasts, tea-soirées, tea-picnics*, *tea-visits*, *tea-dinners*, and even *tea-fights* (a slang term for a tea-party rather than a bun-fight). A great frequenter of such events, assumed to be acting from disreputable motives, was known as a *tea-hound*. The light refreshment taken in the afternoon is still known as *tea*, although in some parts of Britain this is now used to refer to the evening meal. But how many households retain the *tea-bell*, used to summon the family to assemble at the appointed hour?

Although the morning cup of tea can be an essential way of starting the day, there is a range of terms testifying to the dangers of excessive tea-drinking, such as *tea-sot* (*sot* is a word for a drunken fool) and *tea-drunkard*: 'one who habitually drinks tea to such excess as to suffer from its toxic effects'. To be described as *tea-faced* implied a 'sallow or effeminate countenance like one addicted to tea-drinking'. Over-consumption of tea can also be a source of flatulence, as suggested by the origins of the expression 'More tea, Vicar?' used to cover the embarrassment prompted by some social *faux pas* (French for 'false step', referring to an embarrassing or tactless remark). This phrase is supposed to originate in an effort to fill an awkward silence caused by a vicar breaking wind at a tea-party: 'More tea, Vicar?' the genteel hostess asked in a deft attempt to save the clergyman's blushes. But the vicar—unversed in the niceties of social etiquette—responded bluntly: 'No thank you, it makes me fart.'

Tea is usually followed by *breakfast*; this term for the first meal of the day dates from the fifteenth century—the Anglo-Saxons knew it as *forme-mete* 'early food'. Other words have been used over the years; in the eighteenth century, the French word *déjeuner* was adopted into English. Today this refers to lunch in French, while breakfast is known as *petit déjeuner* 'little lunch'—a term initially employed to refer to a light lunch or morning snack. The origins of *déjeuner* are similar to those of *breakfast*, since it is based upon the Latin *de* (a reversative prefix) and *jejunus* 'fasting', literally 'undoing fasting', as *breakfast* means to break one's fast. The Latin word *jejunus* is also the root of *jejune*—originally meaning 'without food', this word came to be used metaphorically to signal something that lacks intellectual nourishment. If you are feeling especially hungry you might opt for a *meat breakfast*, or *fork breakfast*—eighteenth- and nineteenth-century names for what is now usually known as an *English breakfast*, or *full English*. Alternatively you could choose a more traditional option such as *porridge*, although perhaps not in its original form of a thick stew; the word began life as a variant form of *pottage* (from Latin *potagium* 'broth') and only in the seventeenth century started to be used of the oatmeal dish served at breakfast. The frequency with which prisoners were served porridge led to the expression *doing porridge* to refer to time spent in prison, also reflected in the expression *in stir*. Alternatively you may choose to follow the advice of the Egg Marketing Board in the 1960s and *go to work on an egg*.

Eggs

The word *egg* is a borrowing from the Old Norse language; before the Viking invasions, the Anglo-Saxons used the related word *æg* (pronounced 'ay'). The Latin word for egg is *ovum* (plural *ova*) which is the origin of *oval* ('egg-shaped'), *ovary*, *ovulate*, and *Ovaltine* (so called because it consists of dried egg). The egg white also goes by the technical term *albumen*, from Latin *albus* 'white'— also the name given to the white-bearded Albus Dumbledore, headmaster of Hogwarts. The name for the *yolk* also derives from its colour, since it is a form of Old English *geolu* 'yellow'.

The importance of eggs is apparent from the way we categorize people as *good eggs, bad eggs*, and *rotten eggs*. Someone who is unsentimental and ruthless is *hard-boiled*; less commonly, the opposite qualities can prompt the label *soft-boiled*. A particularly difficult person to deal with may be described as a *tough egg to crack*; confronting people like this can leave you feeling as if you are *walking on eggshells*. At all costs you should avoid *teaching your grandmother to suck eggs*—giving someone instruction in something self-evident—especially if she is an *egghead*, a colloquial term for an intellectual. If, in your desire to please, you are guilty of over-embellishing and exaggerating, you may be accused of *over-egging the pudding*. When you find you've had enough you can always *rotten-egg* them—literally, using a method of expressing disdain that has become a regular feature of political protest, or metaphorically, by critiquing or ridiculing someone. Someone prone to interrupting with unfounded rumours and tall stories is said to *come in with five eggs a penny and four of them rotten*; the simplest response to such interventions is: *go suck an egg*!

The importance of eggs to material existence is apparent from the way they feature in expressions concerning future planning. An investment for the future is a *nest egg*; one that is absolutely certain may be *as sure as eggs is eggs*, or *as safe as eggs*; a riskier proposition is *to place all your eggs in one basket*—that is, to bet everything on a single venture. Similar ideas lie behind idioms that are now obsolete. If you are tricked by a conman, you could find yourself being given *eggs for money*—exchanging a thing of value for something worthless. You could retaliate by *breaking the egg in their pocket*, an eighteenth-century expression meaning to spoil someone's plan. But be warned—if your plan goes wrong, you could end up with *egg on your face*.

Should you decide to have an omelette for breakfast you will need to break your eggs, since—as the saying goes—*you can't make an omelette without breaking eggs*. This proverb, recognizing that significant accomplishments generally require some form of sacrifice or adverse effect, is first recorded in the eighteenth century and is based upon an earlier French equivalent: *on ne saurait faire d'omelette sans casser des œufs*. There's no arguing with the logic of this phrase, though it is also true of pretty much any dish made using eggs. Despite appearances, the word *omelette* is unconnected to the eggs from which it is made. Instead, it derives from Latin *lamella* 'thin plate'; this became Old French *alemele*—the additional 'a' was due to confusion as to where the definite article *la* 'the' ended and the word began. This word was used to refer to a thin plate, as in Latin, but also the blade of a knife—from this it came to be used of the egg dish, probably because of its similarly thin, flat shape. The change in the opening vowel from 'a' to 'o' may have been the result of an association with the word *œuf* 'egg'—an association further suggested by the now *defunct* (Latin *defunctus* 'dead') form *œufmelete*.

For a lighter start to the day you could choose a bowl of cereal; made by roasting grain, *cereal* takes its name from Ceres, the Roman goddess of agriculture. Or perhaps you'd prefer a *Continental breakfast*—despite its name, this term usually refers more specifically to the kind of breakfast consumed by the French. Typically, this consists of a loaf of French bread, or *French stick*, known more poetically in French as a *baguette*, meaning 'small rod, wand' (from Latin *baculum* 'staff'). The same word lies behind *imbecile*, which literally means 'without a staff', and was initially used to describe someone who was physically rather than mentally frail. The French stick may be accompanied by *croissants*, from the French word for 'crescent', which take their name from their shape. Both *crescent* and *croissant* go back to Latin *crescens*, meaning 'waxing' or 'growing', which was originally used to describe the period between a new moon and a full moon, when it appears to be growing. It was only later that the word was transferred to objects whose shape resembled that of the moon at this time.

If you want to be genuinely continental you could sample a variety of national delicacies, such as a *waffle*, from a Germanic root meaning 'honeycomb'; *pumpernickel*, a dark rye German bread from *pumper* 'fart' and *Nickel*, a pet form of the name Nikolaus; *bagel*, a Yiddish term that is related to an Old English word for a metal arm-ring; or a *muffin*, rather more prosaically from a Germanic root meaning 'little cake'. The Italian bread known as *focaccia* means 'bread baked in the hearth'; its origins lie in the Latin word *focus* 'hearth, fireplace'. For the Romans the *focus* was the centre of the home—the place where the cooking was done and where the household deity was worshipped. *Focus* was first adopted into English in the seventeenth century as a geometrical term referring to a fixed point from which the distances to any point of a curve are connected; from this it subsequently widened to refer to any centre of interest. Another Italian bread, the *ciabatta*, takes its name from a dialect term for an old shoe with a worn-down heel—a reference to the shape of the loaf.

The plain English *bread* derives from an Old English word, also recorded in other Germanic languages, probably going back to a root meaning 'piece, fragment, morsel', represented in Latin by *frustum*. But this was not the usual term in Old English, which instead preferred *hlaf*—the origin of modern English *loaf*. The importance of this foodstuff to life in Anglo-Saxon England is apparent in the etymology of the words *lord* and *lady*: these derive from Old English *hlaford* 'guardian of the bread' and *hlafdige* 'kneader of the bread'. Now obsolete, but revived briefly in the nineteenth century, is the Old English term *hlafæta* 'loaf-eater', used to describe a household servant who consumes the bread supplied by the lord. A similar explanation lies behind the later coinage *beefeater*, which was used contemptuously of well-fed servants. Bread is central to a number of common English terms and expressions: a *breadwinner* is the person who earns the money to support a family; *to have the bread taken out of one's mouth* is to lose a job. If you *know on which side your bread is buttered*, you are aware of where your interests lie; *to butter one's bread on both sides*, on the other hand, is to be wasteful or overly indulgent. Cockney rhyming slang lies behind the expression *use your loaf*, meaning 'think about it, use your common sense', since *loaf of bread* rhymes with *head*.

The butter that you smear on your bread has changed little from the Old English word *butere*, which is ultimately derived from Greek *bouturon*. Bread and butter is considered such a staple that *having one's bread and butter* signifies the necessities of life, while *to have one's bread buttered for life* suggests that you are set up for the future. The slippery nature of butter has given rise to an association with flattery, as in the verb *butter up*, though such attempts may not always have the desired effect since, as the proverb notes, *fine words butter no parsnips*. Alternatively you may prefer to use *margarine*, which is named after the Greek *margaron* 'pearl'—a reference to the similarity of its appearance to mother-of-pearl. First introduced in the late nineteenth century, *margarine* was originally pronounced with a hard 'g'; the soft sound is recorded from the early twentieth century, paving the way for the more common abbreviated form: *marge*.

You might also wish to add a dollop of a fruit preserve, better known in England as *jam* and in the US as *jelly*—from Latin *gelata* 'frozen', also the root of *congeal*. The name *jam* comes from the verb meaning 'push, squeeze'—a reference to the squashing and pulping involved in the production process. Where bread and butter represent life's necessities, jam has come to signal any kind of additional treat. To *want jam on it* suggests a desire for an easy life, while *money for jam* refers to a cushy assignment with the additional benefit of getting paid. But, be warned, the offer of *jam tomorrow* might sound promising, but instead refers to a promise for the future that is never delivered—a phrase that originates in Lewis Carroll's second Alice novel *Through the Looking-Glass* (1871): 'The rule is, jam to-morrow and jam yesterday—but never jam to-day' (the hyphens in *to-morrow* and *to-day* reminding us that these were originally separate words).

Given the unreliability of jam, it might seem safer to stick to marmalade. Indeed, the popular accounts of its origins suggest that it has medicinal properties, since it is often thought to have been concocted as a medicine for Mary Queen of Scots when she was ill. From *Marie malade* (French for 'ill'), it is alleged, we derived the word *marmalade*. The true origins of the word are rather more straightforward; *marmalade* is derived from quince jam known in Portuguese as *marmelada*—from *marmelo* 'quince', which goes back to Greek *melimelon*, literally 'honey apple'. If you are more Winnie-the-Pooh than Paddington Bear, you might be tempted to reach down the honey pot. *Honey* is a Germanic word in origin, first recorded in Old English as *hunig*—revealing that Pooh bear's spelling *hunny* is actually more authentic than the standard form. Once your bread has been smothered with honey it is literally *mellifluent*—this word, meaning 'pleasant-sounding', is derived from a Latin word meaning 'flowing with honey'.

The more health-conscious, however, might shun these carbohydrates smeared in sugar and instead opt for something fruity—getting a start on the now obligatory five-a-day.

Fruits

Fruits are an essential part of our diet and also of our language. Something we approve of may be a *peach*, a *plum, top banana*, or the *apple of our eye*. Someone we dislike is a *bad apple*, while a particularly difficult character can *drive us bananas*. We can show our disdain for someone by *handing them a lemon*, not *giving a fig*, passing them *the rough end of the pineapple*, or *blowing a raspberry*. While the apple is seen as the key to healthy living—an apple a day keeps the doctor away—it also forms the basis of the names for many fruits. The Greek word for the apple, *melos*, is the origin of *melon*; its Latin equivalent appears in *persicum malum* 'Persian apple'—the source of English *peach*. The Romans also used *pomum* (ancestor of French *pomme*), found in the *pomum granatum* 'many-seeded apple', which gives us the English *pomegranate*.

The word *apple* originates in the Old English *æppel* used by the Anglo-Saxons; related forms appear in all Germanic languages—compare German *Apfel*, Dutch *appel*, and Swedish *äpple*. *Apple* also crops up in the name of fruits that are not apples, such as *pineapple*. Modelled on Latin *pomum pini*, *pineapple* was initially used to refer to the pine cone (as French *pomme de pin* still does); the resemblance of the fruit to the pine cone led to a change in meaning. Many languages instead use a word based upon *nanas* (French *ananas*)—the name given to the fruit in the language of the Tupi people of Peru, where Europeans first encountered the plant. The sixteenth-century *love apple*, a translation of the French *pomme d'amour*, was an alternative name for the tomato—a reference to the fruit's supposed aphrodisiac properties. Modern English *tomato* originates in the Mexican *tomatl*; the change from *tomate* to *tomato* was probably triggered by comparison with *potato* (from Spanish *patata*)—a case of 'you say tomate, I say tomato' perhaps. The sixteenth-century *mad apple*, or *raging apple*, from French *pomme de rage*, was neither an apple nor a tomato, but an aubergine (known in the US as an *eggplant*).

A number of fruits are types of *berry*, from Old English *berie*, used to refer to small roundish fruits without stones. Of the various compounds formed with *berry*, some describe colour—*blackberry, blueberry*—others, such as the *loganberry*, preserve the name of the *horticulturalist* (from Latin *hortus* 'garden') who first cultivated them. Etymologists still puzzle over the first element of *strawberry*; it may refer either to the stalks or the yellow seed-like dots. The *cran* of *cranberry* probably derives from an association with the crane—gooseberry suggests a similarly mysterious connection with the goose—while the *mul* of *mulberry* derives less obscurely from Latin *morum*, the name for the mulberry tree. The first element of *raspberry* originates in the obsolete *raspis*, a collective term for raspberries. Examples like these—where the first element relates to no independent English word—are known to linguists as *cranberry morphemes*.

The *grape* gets its name from a Germanic root meaning 'hook'—referring to the object used to harvest them. *Raisin*, the English term for a dried grape, is borrowed from the French word for grape, itself derived from Latin *racemus* 'bunch of grapes'. The word *currant* originates in the French *raisin de Corinthe* 'grape of Corinth', since currants are the dried fruit prepared from a grape grown in the Levant. Although Old English had the word *ciris*, *cherry* was borrowed from the Northern French dialect word *cherise* (compare the standard modern French form *cerise*). The 's' ending was mistakenly understood to be a plural, and consequently the singular *cherry* was formed.

Although it entered English from Spanish, *apricot* goes back to the Latin word *praecox*, meaning 'early ripening'; this is also the root of *precocious*, used to describe children who are intellectually advanced for their age. The *nectarine* is from the adjectival form of *nectar*, now the sugary fluid secreted by flowers, but originally used in Greek and Roman mythology to refer to the drink of the gods. The food consumed by the classical deities, known as *ambrosia*, is preserved in the French word *framboise* 'raspberry'—from Latin *fraga ambrosia* 'ambrosial strawberry'.

From further afield comes the *orange,* a borrowing from French that has its origins in the Arabic *naranj*; loss of the initial 'n' occurred in French through assimilation with the 'n' of the indefinite article *un*. *Lemon* is also of Arabic origin, although it entered English via the French *limon*, now only used of the lime (*la lime*) in French, which uses *citron* for lemon (the root of English *citric*). *Tangerines* are so called because they originate in the Moroccan port of Tangier, while *satsumas* take their name from the Japanese province in the island of Kyushu. The *mandarin* orange gets its name from the similarity of the pale orange colour of the peel to the yellow silk robes worn by the senior members, or *mandarins* (from Hindi *mantri* 'counsellor'), of the imperial Chinese civil service.

CHAPTER 3

Getting dressed

Once you have breakfasted it's time to get washed and dressed—what was once known rather quaintly as *making one's toilet*. This expression draws upon the origins of the word *toilet*, which was initially a French term for a piece of cloth that served as a cover for a dressing table. The meaning of the word subsequently extended to encompass the objects for making up and arranging the hair stored on a dressing table. In a further extension of the word's meaning it came to encompass the dressing room, and subsequently a room with facilities for washing and relieving oneself (while *toiletries* are now used of the soap, shampoo, and toothpaste used in the washing process). The question of what to call such a room remains a considerable social headache. Since Nancy Mitford popularized the distinction between U (Upper-class) and non-U (non-Upper, i.e. Middle-class) language in the 1950s, speakers wishing to associate with the higher classes have tended to prefer *lavatory* (from Latin *lavare* 'to wash'), *lav*, and *WC* (*Water-Closet*). The Romans themselves opted for a similarly euphemistic term: *lavatrina*, shortened to *latrina*—the root of English *latrine*, the term for a toilet on an army camp. Other *circumlocutory* (from Latin, meaning 'speaking around') terms, particularly favoured in the US, include *smallest room, cloakroom, bathroom,* and *rest room*. The slang term *khazi* was introduced into English via Polari, a secret language developed in the eighteenth and nineteenth centuries among minority groups, drawing upon Italian words, rhyming slang, and other cant terms. *Khazi* is first recorded in the nineteenth century in the forms *carsey* and *carser* and is a borrowing from the Italian *casa* 'house'. The *khazi* spelling, first recorded from the 1970s, is thought to have been influenced by the *Khasi of Khalabar*, a character in the film *Carry On Up the Khyber* (1968). Now let's turn to the business of getting dressed, in order to ensure that you leave the house looking *sartorially* elegant—from *sartor* 'tailor' (from Latin *sarcire* 'to patch').

Clothes

Clothes was originally the plural of *cloth*; alternative, rather old-fashioned, equivalents include *raiment* (an abbreviation of *arrayment*), *attire* (from the Old French verb *atirer* 'equip', from the phrase *à tire* 'in order'), or *apparel* (originally a verb meaning 'make ready, prepare', from French *pareil*, the diminutive of Latin *par* 'equal' and which is adapted into current English in *nonpareil*, 'unequalled'). The traditional method of clothmaking involved weaving, washing (or *fulling*), and drying the woollen cloth—using a wooden frame known as a *tenter* (from Latin *tendere* 'to stretch'). To prevent the cloth from shrinking and creasing, it was attached using *tenterhooks*, adjustable pegs that enabled the material to be held in tension without tearing. It is from this that we get the expression *on tenterhooks* to describe someone who is held in a state of impatience or stress. The Latin word for clothing, or an individual item, was *vestis*—the origin of *vest* and *vestment*, more usually used today of ecclesiastical robes (kept in a *vestry*). As the form might suggest, the word *robe* is connected to the verb *rob* 'steal', since clothing was a target for plundering Germanic tribes. A *habit*, now used of the gown worn by nuns, was originally a general term for clothing, and subsequently the attire associated with a particular profession—from which the religious usage evolved. Deriving from Latin *habere* 'to have', *habit* also came to refer to a person's manner of behaviour and bearing, from which we get the more common modern sense of 'regular practice', or 'behaviour'.

Unless you are a superhero, it's probably most sensible to begin the dressing process with under-garments—also known as *briefs, smalls,* or *scanties.* Although now used of underwear worn by women, *knickers* were originally *knickerbockers,* a kind of short trousers sported by men—especially young boys, since they allowed greater freedom of movement. *Pants* derive from *pantaloons,* named after Pantalone, a character in Italian commedia dell'arte who sported tight trousers. A rather more old-fashioned choice are *bloomers,* named after social reformer Mrs Amelia J. Bloomer (1818–94) who promoted trousers gathered at the ankle as a practical outfit for women. *Bra* is a shortening of *brassière,* originally a French term for a child's vest or *bodice*—the latter word originally a variant form of *bodies* and referring to a form of underclothing.

The term *bluestocking,* used of an intellectual devoted to scholarly pursuits, goes back to an eighteenth-century literary discussion group for women founded by Elizabeth Montagu, Elizabeth Vesey, and others. These literary salons were noted both for their intellectual repartee and for their informality; male participants tended to wear blue worsted stockings rather than the more traditional white silk stockings—hence the name *bluestocking assemblies.*

Despite their different functions today, *shirt* and *skirt* were originally the same word—*shirt* being the Old English form, while *skirt* was borrowed from Old Norse. Both go back to a Germanic root meaning 'short', also found in *shorts.* The *dress* derives from the verb of the same form, which is a borrowing of an Old French verb meaning 'set upright, arrange', from the Latin *directus* 'straight'. *Suit* was initially used of the matching livery worn by members of a royal household or medieval guild. The word is taken from Latin *sequi* 'I follow', referring to the way a suit is a set of items intended to be worn together. The word *livery* comes from Old French *livrer* 'to deliver', a reference to the practice of a household distributing livery to servants, along with provisions. A *jacket* was originally a *jack*, a short protective coat typically worn by French peasants, from the personal name *Jacques*. A *tie* is rather straightforwardly so called because it is tied; less obviously, the *cravat* gets its name from the French word for *Croat*, because the necktie originates in a scarf worn by Croatian mercenaries residing in France.

Jeans are named after the cloth from which they are made, which was originally produced in the Italian city of Genoa. The fabric was originally known as *jean fustian* 'fustian from Genoa', from which the word *jean*—and later *jeans*—derived. Modern jeans were invented by Levi Strauss (1829–1902), hence the alternative name of *Levis*. The cotton cloth from which they are made was originally manufactured in the French town of Nîmes; the fabric's original name, *serge de Nîmes*, is the source of the English name *denim*. Also originating in the name of the fabric from which it was produced is *lingerie*, from French *linge* 'linen'. *Trousers* are of Celtic descent, originating in the singular noun *trouse*, which comes from Scottish Gaelic *triubhas*. Rather more old-fashioned are *breeches*, a word which entered Old English from Latin, where it was used in the singular; since the thirteenth century it has been used of trousers that stop just below the knee. The word's origins share a link with *brogue*, from Gaelic *brog* 'shoe'—originally crude leather shoes worn in the Scottish Highlands, now more usually sported by city commuters. Like breeches are *plus-fours*, originally worn by men for shooting and playing golf in the Edwardian era, which stop just below the knee. The name was coined by cloth-cutters in reference to the additional four inches of material required to allow the distinctive overhang where the end of the trouser meets the sock.

Ensuring that your hair is neatly arranged and your head is covered is crucial if you want to avoid going out looking *dishevelled*, literally 'having the hair uncovered', or *unkempt*, 'uncombed'. Hair standing on end might imply that you are horrified, since *horror* derives from Latin *horrere*, meaning 'to bristle, stand on end'. A similar idea lies behind the word *caprice*, which now refers to a sudden change of mind or behaviour, but which originally referred to a state of terror. The word goes back to an Italian word meaning 'hedgehog head', describing the way that hair standing on end resembles the prickles on a hedgehog.

If you're having a bad-hair day then there's nothing for it but to reach for the hat-stand and try out the latest purchase from your milliner—the technical term for a hat-maker. The word *milliner* goes back to the sixteenth century, when the Italian city of Milan was famous for selling fashionable accessories for women—the original milliners, or *milaners*, were salespeople from Milan.

Hats

Hats are often named after the activity for which they are intended to be worn. A *boater*, or *straw boater*, was—as the name suggests—originally worn for boating, just as a *deerstalker*, made famous by Sherlock Holmes when tracking criminals, was sported when hunting deer. The word *stalk*, meaning 'tread stealthily', is from the same root as the verb *steal*. A *bowler hat*, however, was not devised to be worn while bowling—neither ten-pin nor cricket. It gets its name from its round shape—*bowl* being a variant form of the French *boule* 'ball'—as found in the name of the French form of bowls: *boules*. Its close association with civilian life, as opposed to that of a member of the armed forces, led to its use in expressions referring to the process of demobilization (or *demob*). To leave the forces in the early twentieth century was to be *given one's bowler*, or to be *bowler-hatted*. Another hat that takes its name from its shape is the *cloche hat*—from a French word meaning 'bell'.

The *sombrero* gets its name from the Spanish word *sombra* 'shade', a reference to the protection from the sun offered by its broad brim. A hat with a narrower brim is the *trilby*—named after the title character in a novel by George du Maurier, referring to the soft felt hat worn by an actor in a stage version (the novel also gives us the word *Svengali*, used of a person who exercises a controlling influence over another, after a hypnotist character of that name). The word *bonnet* (from Latin *abonnis* 'headgear') originally referred to a soft hat without a brim sported by men, although today this more usually describes a hat with the brim framing the face and tied under the chin, worn by women and children. The original bonnet resembled the flat woollen hat traditionally worn by members of the Basque peasantry known as a *beret*, which is from the Latin *birrus* 'hooded cape'. This is also the origin of the *biretta*, the square cap worn by members of the Roman Catholic clergy. So, if you're heading off for a day at the Vatican (so called because the papal palace was built on the Vatican Hill in Rome), that should be your headwear of choice.

That headgear can be a marker of social status is apparent from the origins of the word *toff*, signalling a rich person or member of the upper classes. This word is a variation of *tuft*, referring to a tassel of gold that was worn on the hats of members of the nobility when studying at the universities of Oxford and Cambridge. In a similar way, the sixteenth-century practice of soldiers wearing a plume of feathers in their helmets is the origin of the word *panache*. This fashion of sporting a tuft of feathers or *panache*, from Latin *pinnaculum* 'little feather', was adopted by other young men in an attempt to have some of the soldiers' breezy self-confidence rub off on them. From this the word *panache* developed its modern sense of 'flamboyant swagger'.

If it's really bucketing down you will need to avail yourself of an *umbrella*, a diminutive form of Latin *umbra* 'shade'. Someone who is metaphorically under a shade is now described as being *sombre*—from Latin *sub* 'under' and *umbra*. Perhaps I'm being too *pessimistic* (from Latin *pessimus* 'worst'), and it's one of those rare days when the sun is shining. In this case you might prefer to carry a *parasol*—from Italian *parasole* (*para* 'protecting against' and *sole* 'sun').

CHAPTER 4

Commuting

Looking *glamorous* (a word which is related to *grammar*) and suitably attired, it's time to tackle the *commute*. This term for the journey to work was introduced in US English in the 1960s. It originates in the *commutation ticket*; from Latin *com* 'altogether' and *mutare* 'to change', the commutation ticket was a season ticket, in which the daily charge for travel was commuted to a single payment. Instead you may prefer to travel by *car*—from the Latin *carrus* 'wheeled vehicle', or 'wagon'. Perhaps you are sufficiently important to be driven to work in a *limousine*. This may sound grand to us, but its etymological origins are considerably humbler. The limousine gets its name from the French city of Limousin, famous for the production of a hooded cloak favoured by drivers of early automobiles, in which the driver's seat was placed outside. The term *limousine* was subsequently transferred to the cars themselves, especially ones where the chauffeur was separated from the passengers. And while the word *chauffeur* conjures up images of drivers in livery and peaked caps, its origins are also rather less grand. The word derives from the French verb *chauffer* 'to heat', and so means 'stoker'—the person responsible for keeping a steam-engine fully stoked with coal. Given this, you may prefer to drive yourself—an opportunity to show off your sports car, or to roll down the roof of your cabriolet. While *cabriolet* is now a general term for a car with a folding roof, it was originally used of an eighteenth-century two-wheeled carriage with a hood. Because of its tendency to jump up and down on the uneven streets, this vehicle was named using the French verb *cabrioler*, 'to leap in the air'. The origins of this verb lie in the Latin *capra* 'she goat'; the goat's fondness for leaping is also preserved in the word *caper* 'a frolicsome leap', and in the phrase *to cut a caper*. At this time of the morning, though, frolicsome leaps are inadvisable.

Perhaps, in the spirit of cutting congestion on the roads, or doing your bit for the environment, you prefer to use public transport. You could travel by *bus*, a clipped form of the Latin word *omnibus* 'for all' (the same word appears as a prefix in words like *omnivore* and *omniscient*). The word was first employed by a French company which transported its customers between Nantes and a nearby *lido*, or bathing place (from Italian *lido* 'shore'). The name itself was borrowed from a French tradesman called Omnès, whose slogan was *Omnès omnibus* ('Omnès for all'); the idea behind applying this to the transport company was to distinguish it from more expensive, and thus more exclusive, competitors. If your journey requires you to take more than one bus, be warned—despite being a Latin word ending in -*us*, the plural of *omnibus* is not *omnibi*. This is because *omnibus* is the dative plural of *omnes*, and so is already in the plural. Despite this, nineteenth-century spellings do include *omnibi*—as well as the even more egregious *omnibus's*. The original omnibuses were staffed by *omnibus cads*—this sounds like an insult now, since today the word *cad* refers to someone who behaves dishonourably, but it began life as a shortened form of *cadet*. The modern meaning, glossed in *OED* as 'A fellow of low vulgar manners and behaviour', with the important further rider: 'An offensive and insulting appellation' (in case you were thinking of using it as a compliment), developed from Oxford slang for townspeople who did not belong to the university. Buses and coaches may be similar today, but their origins are very different. The original coaches were horse-drawn carriages used for state occasions by the Hungarian royal family in the sixteenth century. Since it was constructed in the town of Kocs, this vehicle was known as *kocsi szekér* 'wagon from Kocs', from which the English word *coach* is derived. Alternatively you might choose to travel by *railway*; although this is now the standard British English term, whereas *railroad* is favoured in US English, the two were widely used in both Britain and the USA when rail travel was first introduced. To get at least a rough idea of when a train will depart you will need to consult a timetable or *schedule*, from a Latin diminutive form of the Greek *skhede* 'papyrus leaf', used in the fourteenth century to mean 'ticket' or 'label'.

Passing the time on the train might involve flicking through a *magazine*—from the Italian *magazzino* 'storehouse', this word was originally used to refer to a warehouse for storing goods or merchandise, or a military arms and ammunition depot (from which the modern sense of receptacle for feeding cartridges into a gun derives). In the eighteenth century *magazine* began to be used of journals and newspapers on specialist topics, such as *The Gentleman's Magazine* or *The Mechanics' Magazine*—the idea being that they were storehouses of information. In the seventeenth century, periodical publications were commonly known by the term *gazette*—as in *The London Gazette* and *The Edinburgh Gazette*. The word *gazette* is also of Italian extraction, originating in the Italian *gazzetta*. This term for a cheap news-sheet goes back to the name of a fifteenth-century Venetian publication known as *gazeta de la novità* 'halfpennyworth of news', so called because it cost a single Venetian coin known as the *gazeta*. Its cheap price and dubious reporting resulted in a somewhat mixed reputation; for a more official account of the news you might prefer to consult a *bulletin*. This word derives from the Italian *bulleta*, meaning 'official warrant, passport', the diminutive of *bulla* 'seal'. *Bulla* is the origin of the papal bull—an edict issued by the pope to which his official seal is attached.

If a papal bull feels a bit heavy for first thing in the morning, or if your Latin is a little rusty, you might prefer something more lightweight. Perhaps you could leaf through a brochure, while pondering your next purchase or holiday. The *brochure* gets its name from the French verb *brocher* 'to stitch'—it literally means 'stitched work'. This is a reference to the way the pages were stitched together rather than being bound, as was customary with a more expensive and finished production. Or perhaps it's time to wade through some of the inevitable office paperwork, household bills, and correspondence—known collectively as *bumf*. This word is rather appropriately a shortening of *bum-fodder*, a nineteenth-century term for toilet paper that was later transferred to other kinds of worthless printed materials. The most etymologically appropriate reading matter to accompany your travels is a journal, since both *journal* and *journey* derive from Latin *diurnalis* 'belonging to a day'. *Journey* was originally a term for the distance that was travelled in a single day (usually considered to be 20 miles), while a *journal* was initially a daily record of events or financial transactions. Perhaps particularly suitable reading matter for a train is a *railway novel*, a nineteenth-century term for a lightweight work of fiction produced in a cheap edition and sold on railway platforms. The word *novel* is from Latin *novus* 'new', and originally referred to any new, or novel, story; *novella* 'short novel' is the diminutive form. For variety you could choose an *anthology*—etymologically a collection of flowers, from Greek *anthos* 'flower'. The reason behind the name is that an anthology was considered to be a collection of the finest authors, or flowers of literature.

Books

The word *book* is probably related to the name of the beech tree, perhaps because the earliest forms of Germanic writing were scratched onto wood. These messages would have been carved using the ancient Germanic writing system known as *runes*: from an Old English word that can also mean 'secret'. Runic characters are formed using a series of angular strokes, avoiding the loops found in many of our modern letters, since they were specifically developed for scratching onto hard surfaces: stones, bone, wood, and deer-horn. For us there is an obvious connection between the name of a tree like the beech and the word *book*, since the paper from which books are made today comes from the sap drawn from trees. But this connection does not apply for much of the medieval period since paper was only introduced to England in the fifteenth century, and even then in the form of a paper made from rags. Paper was first developed by the Chinese in the second century AD; it took a millennium before it made its way via the Arab world to western Europe. The word *paper* points back to a much earlier form of book-making, since it comes from the word *papyrus*, the writing material prepared by the ancient Egyptians using the pithy stem of a water plant. Papyrus was still known in the early Middle Ages, but fell out of use in the seventh century since it was too fragile to be used in books. The introduction of paper led to the adoption of watermarks—an image that was incorporated into the paper during manufacture that identified its maker. One such maker's mark, a fool's cap, lies behind the use of *foolscap* to refer to paper of a certain size. During the Middle Ages, texts were written on animal skin—in England sheepskin (known as *parchment*—from Latin *pergamina* 'writing material from Pergamum', a city in the west of Turkey where the material was thought to have been invented) was particularly common, though the more expensive deerskin (*vellum*, from vitellus 'little calf'—also the root of *veal*) was used for more *deluxe* (French 'of luxury') productions. Medieval manuscripts are so called because they were written by hand: Latin *manu* 'by hand' and *scriptus* 'written'; the Latin *scribere* 'to write' also lies behind the words *scribe* and *script*. The writing implement was a quill pen fashioned out of a bird's feather (*quill* is from a Germanic root meaning 'shaft of a feather'); it is for this reason that the word *pen* originates in the Latin *penna* 'feather'. The end of the quill was cut to form a *nib*—a variant of the Old English *neb*, used of a bird's beak or a person's nose—using a *pen-knife*; this is the origin of the term for an implement more usually associated today with boy scouts and members of the Swiss army.

Wood did, however, play a part in the construction of a book in the Middle Ages, since it was the main material used in bookbindings. Although the words *book* and *beech* don't appear connected today, the relationship is clearer if we go back to Old English. That's because the plural of the Old English word *book* was *bec*, pronounced 'beech': it was one of a group of plurals where the stem vowel changed instead of adding an ending. Some of these survive into modern English—think of *tooth–teeth, foot–feet*—but most have become regularized according to the dominant class of nouns which form their plural by adding an 's'. The word *book* appears in a range of compounds in Old English: a letter was a *bocstæf* (literally 'book-character'), and a library was a *bochus* 'book-house'. As with much of the vocabulary of modern English (especially in the more technical fields), these words have mostly been replaced with words borrowed from Latin. Old English *bocstæf* is now a *letter* (from Latin *littera*); *bochus* has been replaced by *library* (from the Latin word *liber* 'book'). The Latin word *liber* has a similar etymology to the English word *book*, since it originated in the Latin word for the bark of a tree. Like many Latin words now used in English, *library* entered the English language from French (which is itself derived from Latin); however, in adopting the word, English speakers introduced an important change in meaning. In French *librairie* meant bookseller's shop, while in English, *library* referred to a place set apart for public study and reference of books. This distinction still applies, and is one to bear in mind if you should ever find yourself tempted to walk off with a book from a French *librairie*. The word for library in French is *bibliothèque*, which draws upon the Greek word for book—*biblos*—originally the name for the papyrus plant, and the origin of the English word *Bible*.

The connection between *book* and the Bible is an important one, since the first Bibles represent the earliest instances of the *codex*—the Latin word for a book, a variant form of *caudex* 'trunk of a tree'—the form of the book as we know it. *Codex* is also the root of the words *code* and *codify*—the process of arranging and compiling a set of rules or laws according to an authoritative system. Before the birth of the codex, texts were inscribed onto wooden *tablets* (from Latin *tabula*, a flat piece of wood—also the root of *table*) coated with wax, onto which messages were scratched using a small pointed rod termed a *stilus*—the modern spelling *stylus* is the result of a mistaken association with the Greek word *stulos*, meaning 'column'. The idiosyncratic features of a person's handwriting were linked with mode of expression and manner of composition, and from this developed the word *style*. Although wooden tablets have been superseded, the word *tablet* is still used today to refer to a reading device, albeit one that is rather more technologically sophisticated. In the era of electronic tablets and smartphones, the stylus has also enjoyed something of a revival, since it is the term used for the pen-shaped device used for writing or drawing on the screen. The Roman *stilus* was blunted at the other end, allowing a message to be rubbed out and the tablet to be re-inscribed. The phrase *tabula rasa*, literally meaning 'scraped tablet' (compare *razor*), referring metaphorically to the human mind at the time of birth, or a state unencumbered by preconceived ideas, draws upon this image of a wax tablet that has been scraped blank ready for re-use. A more modern equivalent term is *blank slate*—deriving from the use of slates as writing surfaces by schoolchildren. Perhaps the next stage will be the formatted iPad.

Wax tablets were suitable only for the recording of short texts and messages; before the codex, longer works were copied onto *scrolls* or *rolls*—this form of book production is the source of modern English *volume*, from Latin *volvere* 'to roll'. A major advantage of the codex format is the ability to flick through its component *pages* (from the Latin *pagina* 'page'—ultimately from the verb *pangere* 'fix, compose'), or *leaves*—a metaphorical reference to the similarities between the pages of a book and the leaves of a tree. This comparison also lies behind the word *folio* 'leaf of paper or parchment', which is from the Latin *folium* 'leaf' (also the root of the English word *foliage*). Latin *folio* is the source of the French word *feuille*, which can also refer to both a leaf on a tree and a page of a book. In a book, the *text* (from the Latin *texere* 'to weave'—reflecting the woven appearance of the script used in medieval manuscripts) is organized into *chapters*. The chapter has its origins in Latin *capitulum*, the diminutive form of *caput* 'head'—referring to the chapter as a smaller division within a larger work. The connection between this and a monastic chapter—the term for a general meeting of the members of a religious community—comes from the practice of reading a chapter of the monastic rule, or of the Bible, at such meetings, in the room that came to be known as the *chapter house*.

In order to navigate lengthy texts, various reading aids have developed. In the medieval period passages of significance were marked using a *manicule* (the diminutive of Latin *manus* 'hand')—a small hand with a finger pointing at the relevant passage. This same image of a guiding finger lies behind the word *index*, which originates in the Latin *index* 'forefinger' (still used in English *index finger*)—also the root of *indicate*. The *appendix*, added at the end of a volume, offering supplementary but not essential information, is from Latin *appendere*, a verb that describes something additional as if it were hung on (like an *appendage*). Turning to the back cover of a modern book we find the *blurb*, a short description of the contents—typically *eulogistic* (from Greek *eulogia* 'praise') and inevitably labelling the book a *bestseller*, originally a nineteenth-century term for anything that outsells its competitors, but now most commonly used of books. *Blurb* was invented by Gelett Burgess (1866–1951), from the depiction of a young woman called Miss Belinda Blurb who featured on the cover of one of his comic books. Burgess offered a definition which neatly captured the content of such descriptive accounts, which are typically 'abounding in agile adjectives and adverbs, attesting that this book is the "sensation of the year"'.

Booksellers were originally known as *stationers* because they operated out of a shop or stall that enjoyed a fixed location (from Latin *statio* 'I stand')—also the root of *stationary*. Early stationers were also engaged in the production of books and in trade in the requisite materials—paper, pens, and ink; from this the modern concept of the *stationer*, dealing exclusively in office and writing materials, arose in the seventeenth century. Printing was introduced to England in the fifteenth century by William Caxton (*c.*1422–*c.*1491), who set up his print shop in Westminster—the centre of the thriving trade in manuscript books. Books printed in this early period—before the beginning of the sixteenth century—are known today as *incunabula* (singular *incunabulum*), a Latin word meaning 'cradle'—a reference to this period as the infancy of printing technology. Caxton brought with him apprentices trained in the Low Countries, where printing was first invented, and this led them to introduce certain Dutch spelling practices: the 'h' added to *ghost* (the Old English form was *gast*) was suggested to them by the Middle Dutch spelling *gheest*. Several other examples, like *ghest* 'guest', *ghoos* 'goose', *gherle* 'girl', also appear in early printed books but then fell out of general use. Because the *majuscule* (Latin for 'somewhat greater') and *minuscule* ('somewhat smaller'—related to *minus* rather than *mini*, hence the spelling) letters were stored in cases at different heights, these came to be known as *upper-case* and *lower-case* letters. Upper-case letters are also known as *capital* letters; this term, yet another derivation from Latin *caput* 'head', was originally used of an ornamented initial appearing at the head of a passage in a manuscript. As well as being decorated, such letters could contain illustrations depicting characters or events in the text, or even, in some cases, the author. The word *author* is from Latin *auctor* 'originator', and in the Middle Ages it was only applied to famous classical writers like Virgil, Ovid, and Homer. Writers like these were considered to carry *authority*, while English writers like Chaucer were viewed as lacking such status, writing not in Latin or Greek but in the *vernacular*. This term is from Latin *vernaculus* 'domestic, indigenous', from *verna*, the word for a native-born slave, referring to the use of an indigenous (from Latin *indigena* 'native') tongue rather than one of the more highly regarded classical languages. Because manuscript illustrations were painted with the red lead known in Latin as *minium*, they came to be known as *miniatures*. Since these pictures were necessarily of reduced size, the term *miniature* came to be extended to refer to all small pictures, and subsequently to any item that is a reduced version of the original.

Instead of reading a book you could purchase a newspaper—either a *broadsheet*—originally a single sheet of paper similar to a *broadside*—or a *tabloid*, from *tablet*—a reference to the paper's small, concentrated, and easily digestible format. Once you have had enough of the gloomy news and celebrity gossip, why not turn to the back page and tackle the ultimate challenge in word puzzles: the cryptic crossword? The crossword was the invention of Liverpool émigré Arthur Wynne, whose first puzzle appeared in the *New York World* in 1913. This initial foray was christened a *Word-Cross*; the instruction in subsequent issues to 'Find the missing cross words' led to the birth of the *crossword*. Solving the daily crossword has long been associated with train travel; in 1920s America, trains between Baltimore and Ohio were supplied with dictionaries as an aid to the growing numbers of *solvers, solutionists, puzzle-heads,* and *cruciverbalists* (Latin for 'crossworders', albeit a twentieth-century formation). In Britain the stereotype of the respectable commuter, attired in pinstripe suit and bowler hat, includes the ability to dispatch the *Times* crossword before arriving at Waterloo.

Crosswords

Crosswords consist of a grid made up of black and white boxes, in which the answers, also known as *lights*, are to be entered. The term *light* derives from the word's wider use to refer to facts or suggestions which help to explain, or *cast light upon*, a problem. The puzzle consists of a series of *clues*, a word that derives from Old English *cleowen* 'ball of thread'. Since a ball of thread could be used to help guide someone out of a maze—just as Ariadne's thread came to Theseus' aid in the Minotaur's labyrinth—it developed the figurative sense of a piece of evidence leading to a solution, especially in the investigation of a crime. The spelling changed from *clew* to *clue* (along with *blew*, *glew*, and *trew*) under the influence of French in the seventeenth century.

In the earliest crosswords the clue consisted of a straightforward *synonym* (Greek 'with name')—this type is still popular in *concise* or *quick* crosswords. A later development saw the emergence of the *cryptic* clue (from a Greek word meaning 'hidden'), where, in addition to a definition, another route to the answer is concealed within a form of wordplay. Wordplay devices include the *anagram*, from a Greek word meaning 'write anew', and the *charade*, from a French word referring to a type of riddle in which each syllable of a word, or a complete word, is described, or acted out—as in the game *charades*. Punning on similar-sounding words, or *homophones* (Greek 'same sound'), is a common trick. A reference to *Spooner* requires a solver to transpose the initial sounds of two or more words; this derives from a supposed predisposition to such slips of the tongue in the speech of Reverend William Archibald Spooner (1844–1930), Warden of New College, Oxford, whose alleged *Spoonerisms* include a toast to 'our queer dean' and upbraiding a student who 'hissed all his mystery lectures'. Other devious devices of misdirection include reversals, double definitions, containers (where all or part of a word must be placed within another), and words hidden inside others, or between two or more words. In the type known as *&lit.* (short for '& literally'), the whole clue serves as both definition and wordplay.

Although crosswords are generally a solitary pastime, the solver enters into battle with the *compiler*, or *setter*, who traditionally remains *anonymous* (Greek 'without name'), or assumes a *pseudonym* (Greek 'false name'). Famous exponents of this dark art include Torquemada (Edward Powys Mathers) and Ximenes (Derrick Macnutt), who adopted the names of Spanish inquisitors, Afrit, the name of a mythological Arabic demon hidden in that of the setter A.F. Ritchie, and Araucaria, the Latin name for the monkey puzzle tree, adopted by the Reverend John Graham. Colin Dexter, inventor of the famous crossword-solving sleuth Inspector Morse, set crosswords for the *Oxford Times* newspaper under the pseudonym Codex (hidden in the name COlin DEXter). Dexter was for many years a regular entrant in the *Observer* newspaper's cryptic clue-writing competition. Inspector Morse and Sergeant Lewis take their names from two of Dexter's principal rivals in that contest—Sir Jeremy Morse (former chairman of Lloyds Bank) and Mrs B. Lewis. In fact all the characters in the first Morse novel, *Last Bus to Woodstock* (1975), with the exception of the murderer, are named after Dexter's crosswording comrades. Morse's first name remains a secret throughout the series; in the penultimate novel, *Death Is Now My Neighbour* (1996), Morse revealed that he was named Endeavour—now the title of a prequel based on Morse's early career—after Captain Cook's ship. In the TV adaptation Morse hints at his name using a cryptic crossword clue: 'My whole life's effort has revolved around Eve': an anagram ('revolved') of around Eve = Endeavour, defined as 'My whole life's effort'.

It is unfortunate that Lewis Carroll (the *nom de plume*, literally 'feather, or quill, name', of Charles Lutwidge Dodgson, 1832–1898), the inventor of several word games and a compulsive re-arranger of letters, died before the crossword was invented, as he would have undoubtedly been a brilliant exponent. Given that, it seems fitting that a key principle of the setter's art—'You need not mean what you say, but you must say what you mean'—is a version of Alice's confusing encounter with the March Hare; while Alice's bewildered response echoes the sentiments of many novices when first confronted with a cryptic clue:

'You should say what you mean,' the March Hare went on.

'I do,' Alice hastily replied; 'at least—at least I mean what I say— that's the same thing, you know.'

'Not the same thing a bit!' said the Hatter. 'Why, you might just as well say that "I see what I eat" is the same thing as "I eat what I see"!' . . .

Alice felt dreadfully puzzled. The Hatter's remark seemed to her to have no sort of meaning in it, and yet it was certainly English.

PART II

Work

CHAPTER 5
The office

For many people the place of work is an *office*, a word which originates in Latin *officium*, referring to an act of service—comprising the words *opus* 'work' and *facere* 'to do'. In the fifteenth century, if you were very effective at carrying out the duties of your office you were considered *officious*—it was in the sixteenth century that this word developed *pejorative* (from Latin *peior* 'worse') connotations, suggesting someone who was interfering and *pompous* (originally meaning 'magnificent, splendid', this word has suffered a similar downgrading). If your office is particularly posh it may be termed a *bureau*. This is a borrowing of a French word for the baize cloth that covered a table, especially one used for accounting or writing. From this, *bureau* came to be used of the writing desk itself—as it still is in French—and subsequently of the room in which the desk is found.

If you share an office with your co-workers, your colleagues are your *chums* and *comrades*, since both words originate in the idea of co-habitation. *Chum* is a shortening of *chamber-fellow*; it first appeared as a slang term for a room-mate among students at the University of Oxford. *Chamber* is ultimately from Latin *camera* 'vaulted ceiling', via the French form *chambre*; from this same source we get *comrade*—originally used of soldiers who shared a tent. Some offices are open-plan, while in others workers are distributed into individual cubicles. If you are fortunate enough to occupy your own cubicle, you should feel at liberty to assume a reclining position and perhaps catch up on a little sleep—*cubicle*, from Latin *cubare* 'to lie down', was originally a bedroom. This sense survives in the word *concubine* 'mistress'—literally someone you lie down with.

Getting too intimate with your colleagues, however, can lead to *cronyism*—the practice of making appointments to positions of responsibility based upon friendship rather than merit. This word, and the related *crony*, are from *khronios* 'long-lasting', referring to friends that you've known for a long time. This Greek word also lies behind *chronic*—a chronic illness, therefore, is strictly speaking one that has lingered for a long time. But today the word is used more loosely to describe a complaint that is simply 'bad' or 'unpleasant', much to the chagrin of those who like to keep their Greek etymologies intact. Related to cronyism is the concept of *Buggins's turn*, referring to an appointment made by rotation, and therefore based upon length of service rather than suitability for the position. This is not to be confused with *muggins*, originally a term for a fool and now employed jocularly to refer to oneself, in situations like: 'Who do you think ended up doing it? Muggins!' Appointing a relative to a post is known as *nepotism*, from Latin *nepos* 'nephew'. The particular focus on nephews, rather than some other family member, derives from the word's original use to describe the special favours that were granted by popes to their nephews, who were often in reality their illegitimate sons.

Attempts to ingratiate yourself with your boss in the hope of advancement risk your being accused of being a *toady*, or a *sycophant*. The word *toady* is a shortening of *toad-eater*, a seventeenth-century term for the assistant to a bogus physician selling dubious concoctions claimed to cure all ills. These *charlatans* (from Italian *ciarlatano* 'babbler, prattler') would attempt to convince prospective customers of the efficacy of their wares by getting their assistant to consume the remedy and then eat (or at least make a pretence of eating) a toad—thought at that time to be poisonous. The parallel term *sycophant* has an equally colourful etymology. It originates in a Greek word used of an informer, literally meaning 'one who shows the fig' (from Greek *sukon* 'fig'). There have been a number of attempts to explain the connection between fig-showing and sneaking. One possibility is that the term arose from the practice of informing on those who illegally traded in figs. Perhaps more likely is that it refers to some obscene gesture known as making a fig, similar to giving someone the finger, or (in Shakespeare's day) biting your thumb at someone. Because of the way in which informing on someone (also known as *snitching, grassing,* and *dobbing in*) can be used as a means of ingratiating yourself with a boss, the term *sycophant* developed its modern sense of flatterer. To *kowtow,* describing the obsequious and servile behaviour demonstrated by some towards their bosses, is from a Chinese word meaning 'knock the head', referring to the practice of prostrating oneself so that the forehead touches the ground, as a demonstration of submission and respect.

It may be that, despite all this toadying and sycophancy, your boss is *surly* towards you. This word was originally spelled *sirly* and literally meant 'like a sir'—a reference to the overbearing and pompous behaviour typically displayed by someone who was a *sir* to the lower orders, and could therefore *lord it over* them. The tendency for those of the higher classes to look down on their inferiors is also captured by *haughty,* a well-disguised form of Latin *altus* 'high' (via French *haut*)—the silent 'gh' was added in the sixteenth century by comparison with *caught* and *taught.* The Latin word for arrogant and haughty was *superciliosus*—the root of the English *supercilious.* This word is derived from *supercilium,* the Latin term for an eyebrow (from *super* 'above' and *cilium* 'eyelid')—the idea being that raising the eyebrow is a means of communicating disdain. This association is also captured in the phrase *raise an eyebrow,* an expression referring to an understated demonstration of mild surprise, scepticism, or disapproval. The idea that a person's character is reflected in the face is apparent in the word *highbrow,* referring to someone who is highly intelligent and cultured, or to something intellectually challenging; the term originated in a literal reference to a person with a considerable distance between the eyes and the hairline. Should you feel under attack from your boss or colleagues, you might choose to fight back by *casting aspersions* about them. Originally referring simply to the sprinkling of water around the place (from Latin *spargere* 'to sprinkle'—also the root of *disperse* and *intersperse*), this phrase later came to be used of sprinkling other less welcome substances, such as mud or dung; from this developed the association of the phrase with ruining somebody's reputation.

While no doubt many of us work principally for the enjoyment and satisfaction of a job well done, there is the additional incentive of an *emolument* (originally a payment to a miller for grinding corn, from Latin *emolere* 'to grind up') or pay cheque. The word *salary* is derived from Latin *salarium*, the term for the payment received by Roman soldiers. This word has its origins in *sal* 'salt'—not because the soldiers were paid in salt, but probably reflecting how the money was spent. The connection between providing a service and being rewarded in salt lies behind the expression *to be worth one's salt*—to be efficient and reliable. Those who demonstrate particular integrity may be described as *the salt of the earth*, after a Biblical usage recorded in St Matthew's Gospel (from Old English *god* 'good' and *spel* 'news'). The word *wage* is a Norman French borrowing, a dialectal variant of the Central French *gage*, although it is ultimately of Germanic origin. Its original meaning was 'pledge' or 'security'; it is related to another Germanic word, *wed*, which initially referred to any kind of pledge or promise, but now refers specifically to a *marital* pledge (from Latin *maritus* 'husband').

Money

The word *money* was borrowed from Old French *moneie*, itself from the Latin word for money, or a mint—the place where money is coined—*moneta*. Moneta was the name of a pre-Roman goddess who came to be identified with the Roman goddess Juno; the name was used of Roman currency because it was minted in a temple dedicated to the goddess Moneta. The word *coin* is from Latin *cuneus* 'wedge', a reference to the wedge-shaped die with which the coins were stamped; from *cuneus* we also get *cuneiform*, the name of an ancient Sumerian writing system in which wedges were carved into clay tablets. The engraving tool or die-stamp used to mark impressions upon coins was known to the Greeks as *kharakter*, from which we get *character*—initially used to refer to an identifying token or feature, it subsequently came to signal the distinctive trait of a human personality. The *purse* in which you keep your loose change is from Greek *bursa* 'ox hide', and is the root of *bursar* and *purser*. Larger sums might be stashed in a box, Latin *capsa*, which is the root of *cash*. The importance of animals to financial security is reflected in the origin of Latin *pecunia* 'money' in *pecu* 'flock, herd'; *pecunia* is the source of English *pecuniary*, 'relating to money', and *impecunious* 'lacking money'— also known as *fundless, unpennied, skint, stony-broke, strapped, on the beach*, and *oofless*. The slang use of *oof* for money explains the nickname of the P. G. Wodehouse character Oofy Prosser, the wealthiest member of the Drones Club. A similar link between livestock and money can be traced in *chattel*, an archaic word meaning 'wealth'—preserved in the legal phrase *goods and chattels*, the collective term for personal possessions—which is from the same root as *cattle*.

The main unit of English currency is the *pound*—a Germanic word borrowed from Latin *pondo*, meaning 'by weight'—a reference to the way that the weight of the coin reflected its actual value. The Romans used *pondo* as an abbreviation for *libra pondo* 'a pound weight'; this was misunderstood such that the word for the weight was borrowed into Germanic with the meaning 'pound'. As a consequence, the Germanic languages use variants of the word *pound*, as in German *Pfund* and Dutch *pond*, while Romance languages employ forms derived from Latin *libra*—as in French *livre* and Italian *libbra*. But while English did not adopt the Latin *libra*, it does employ an abbreviation that is taken from this word, since the symbol '£' is based on a capital 'L'; this replaces an earlier usage in which a lower-case 'l' was added after the amount. This origin also helps to explain why the use of *pound* to refer to a unit of weight equal to twelve ounces is abbreviated to *lb*—another abbreviation of Latin *libra*. In England the pound was originally a pound weight of silver, represented by a gold sovereign, and equal in value to 20 shillings or 240 pence. The word *penny* can be traced back to Old English *pæning*, which probably represents a base followed by the '-ing' ending signalling 'belong to', or 'possessed of the quality of'. The meaning and origins of the base are unclear; it may be a borrowing of Latin *pondus*, or is perhaps related to *pan*, the modern English word for a metal cooking vessel, or *pawn*, a borrowing from Middle French *pan* 'pledge, surety'—the origin of modern English *pawnshop* and *pawnbroker*. In the pre-decimal age *penny* and *pence* were abbreviated to 'd'—based upon the initial letter of the ancient Roman coin known in Latin as the *denarius*. English currency is sometimes accompanied by the further descriptive term *sterling*. This word is of uncertain origin, but the *OED* offers the plausible suggestion that it derives from an unattested Old English word *steorling* (from Old English *steorra* 'star') meaning 'coin with a star'—since this was a feature of some of the early Norman coins.

English is rich in slang terms for money; these include *nicker, bread, dough, moolah, spondulicks*, and *quid*. *Quid* can be traced back to the seventeenth century, when it was used with reference to a sovereign; its origins may lie in the Latin *quid* 'what', used in this context to refer to financial means. This use may owe something to the earlier phrase—still in use today—*quid pro quo* 'one thing for another', implying the kind of exchange that is involved in purchasing something using money. This idea of exchange, and of money flowing from one party to another, lies behind the word *currency*—originally referring to anything that flows (like the *current* of a river), ultimately derived from Latin *currentem* from *currere* 'to run'.

To thrive in an office environment you will need to speak the *lingo* (from Latin *lingua* 'language, tongue', originally used of a language that sounds strange or unintelligible)—that is, be able to decode and employ the jargon and buzzwords that are liberally bandied about during any business meeting, or when working through any *agenda* (a Latin word meaning 'things to be done'). The whole point of such terminology is to sound as if you know what you are talking about when you don't. This function is implicit in the etymology of the word *jargon* itself, which is from a medieval French word used to refer to the chattering of birds, and subsequently to speech that is nonsensical or unintelligible.

Business Jargon

One function of business jargon is to make the mundane and frequently uninspiring world of the board room seem more exciting and enticing. To that end it imports phrases that originate in other, more glamorous contexts, such as the world of sport. A major decision might be termed a *game-changer*—originally a US sporting term for a player who decisively affects the outcome of a game. To *touch base*, now used of a short meeting to catch up with someone, originates in the baseball term for making contact with the base during play. Also from baseball is the now ubiquitous phrase *step up to the plate*. A baseball term meaning 'enter the batter's box to take a turn at batting', this has come to refer to the assumption of responsibility for some particular challenge or crisis. Drawing on the pivotal role of the quarterback in a game of American football, *quarterbacking* is an increasingly popular term for the process of directing or organizing an operation. Analysing or critiquing a process in retrospect is known as *armchair quarterbacking*. A particular area of responsibility may be called a *swim lane*; perhaps it is from this that the importance of *getting one's ducks in a row*—ensuring one is well prepared—emerged. Elite athletes who have trained and practised so rigorously that they can respond to any situation in a game without having to pause to think is the source of *no-brainer*—now an idea that is sufficiently self-evident as to require no discussion.

Another fruitful source of business talk is the metaphor of the ball game—your boss may *bowl you a curve ball, play hardball, knock the ball into your court*, expect you to be *on the ball, get the ball rolling, play ball,* and *keep the ball in the air*. In order to ensure fair play you need to maintain a *level playing-field*. If you find yourself getting irritated by discussion of some particular issue, you could employ another sporting idiom and *kick it into touch*—thereby postponing the pain to some later date; for an even more effective deferment, you might prefer to *boot it into the long grass*—with the added benefit that it might get forgotten altogether.

Another fashionable source of business jargon are terms borrowed from new technologies; a way of making us feel we are part of the hip world of Silicon Valley, or—more cynically—a company's way of treating its human workforce as if they were machines. In response to an excessive workload someone might complain that they don't have the *bandwidth* to deal with it, while a discussion to be continued outside a meeting might be *taken offline*. For those who are less up to date with the technological references, there's always the phrase *it's on my radar*, used to describe something of which one is aware. *Radar*, incidentally, began life as an acronym— it comprises the opening letters of *radio detection and ranging*. Also from the world of aviation we get *push the envelope*—a phrase which derives from the use of *envelope* to refer to the combination of speed and altitude within which a plane can safely fly. To *push the envelope* is to stretch this to the extreme of an aircraft's capacity. A group of experts brought in to advise on a particular problem may be referred to as a *SWAT team*—originally a term for a group of elite marksmen summoned to deal with the most dangerous situations (from the initial letters of *Special Weapons and Tactics*), but in a corporate context more typically a collection of middle-aged men in suits.

Brainstorming meetings are ones in which a group attempts to solve a particular issue by floating spontaneous solutions—a key principle of such forums is the dubious assertion that 'there's no such thing as a bad idea'. An anxiety concerning the political correctness of this term, which was considered potentially offensive to epileptics, led Tunbridge Wells Borough Council to ban it, requiring its staff to replace it with the term *thought-shower*. An attempt to enhance such interactions using comfortable and colourful surroundings is known as a *right-brain meeting*—a reference to the association of the right *hemisphere* (Greek *hemi* 'half') of the brain with creativity. In such environments *blue-sky thinking* is encouraged. This phrase, first recorded in the 1920s, was initially employed in the strictly negative sense of 'fanciful', 'hypothetical', 'not practical'. As it came to refer to thinking that didn't necessarily have any immediate pay-off or definite commercial goal, it came to be used positively to mean 'creative', 'visionary', and 'unconstrained by conventional applications'. Such meetings also encourage *thinking outside the box*, an idiom that refers to creative solutions that go beyond the limits of conventional and orthodox approaches. This phrase is first recorded as *thinking outside the dots*, referring to a puzzle which requires the solver to connect a series of dots set out on a square grid with continuously drawn straight lines; to solve the puzzle you need to literally think outside the box—since the lines must be drawn outside the edge of the grid.

Perhaps you have avoided office life entirely, and instead engage in some form of *manual* (from Latin *manus* 'hand') labour. Farming used to be known as *husbandry*—from an archaic sense of *husband* to refer to someone responsible for the management of a household; this term survives mostly as *animal husbandry*, referring to the breeding and care of animals. The word *farm* is connected to *firm*— both ultimately go back to Latin *firmus* 'constant'. From this, medieval Latin *firma* came to be used of a fixed payment, which was used in English to refer to a set annual rent paid by a farmer in exchange for the right to till a piece of land. Land is divided up by the *acre*, from an Old English word for a plot of cultivated land, or a measure of land based upon the extent that could be ploughed by a yoke of oxen in a single day. *Acre* has cognates in many Germanic languages and goes back to the same root that lies behind Latin *ager* 'field' and *agere* 'to act'. It is also the source of the word *acorn*, which originally referred to any fruit that grew in open land or forest. Its meaning was subsequently narrowed to refer only to the fruit of the oak tree; the shift from *æcern* to *acorn* was the result of a popular association of the word with the oak—further apparent from additional recorded spellings such as *ocorn, oakehorn*, and *okehorn*.

Plumbers get their name from the Latin *plumbum* 'lead', since the pipes that carry water, heating, and sanitation used to be constructed from that metal. This word is also the origin of the chemical symbol Pb, as found on the Periodic Table. Someone who works with wood is known as a *carpenter*, a word that goes back to the Gaulish word *carpentum*, meaning 'wagon'. The term *electrician* is from Latin *electrum* 'amber'; since rubbing amber was observed to produce static electricity, *electric* was used to refer to objects that showed similar properties. A *janitor* is now a caretaker tasked with maintaining the upkeep of a building, especially a school. But originally it described a door-keeper or porter—as is implied by its etymology, since it is derived from Latin *janua* 'door, entrance'. Latin *janua* is related to the name of the Roman god Janus, the gatekeeper of heaven, whose image was traditionally placed over doorways, with a face on both the front and back of his head. The month of *January* is also named after Janus, since he watched over the beginning of the new year. *Fireman* has now been replaced by the unisex *firefighter*—a term that goes back to the early nineteenth century, when it replaced the colourful alternative *fire-quencher*, and the French borrowing *pompier* (from *pompe* 'pump').

Since there are many different forms of gainful employment, the following chapters will focus on just a selection of these, covering a variety of jobs within the police and armed forces, the law, the Church, politics, and the health services. Although not many of us are called to be admirals, bishops, or judges, most of us find ourselves interacting with these professions at some point in our lives.

CHAPTER 6

Law and order

The police force takes its name from Latin *politia* 'government', a word which goes back to Greek *polis* 'city'—from which we also get *policy*. Among many nicknames for the police is the term *Old Bill*. This name originates in a cartoon character of a complaining Cockney soldier created by Bruce Bairnsfather (1888–1959) during the First World War. The character was later adopted by the Metropolitan Police, dressed in police uniform, on recruitment posters, leading to the employment of the term as a name for the force. The nineteenth-century detectives replaced the *peelers*, the first London constables, who drew their name from the British politician Sir Robert Peel, who was responsible for their introduction in 1829 when he was Home Secretary. Although the term *peeler* has not survived, we still use *bobby* (coined in allusion to Peel's Christian name) to refer to the humble policeman on the *beat*—a term for the route walked while on duty. Before the peelers, the London streets were patrolled by the Bow Street Runners (1749–1839).

The lowest-ranking police officer is the *constable*; borrowed from French, this term represents the Latin *comes stabuli*, meaning 'count of the stable'—referring to the head officer tasked with the upkeep of the horses. The shift from chief groom to a principal officer in a household, and subsequently to a military commander, is paralleled by *marshal*, discussed below. Names for other police ranks are fairly self-explanatory: *inspector* is from Latin *inspicere* 'to look into'; *superintendent* is from Latin *superintendere* 'to supervise'; *commander* from Latin *commandare* 'to command'; and *commissioner* from Latin *committere* 'entrust' (also the source of *commit*). Officers who are members of the CID (Criminal Investigation Department) have the word *detective* added before their rank.

Detective, originally *detective policeman* (from Latin *detegere* 'to uncover'), was first used to refer to someone whose job it was to solve a crime using methods of surveillance and close investigation in the nineteenth century. This was the period in which the detective novel was born, memorably labelled the age of 'detective fever' by Wilkie Collins, author of *The Moonstone* (1868), one of the earliest and finest whodunnits. The novel features Sergeant Cuff, a template for many of the most famous fictional detectives; Cuff was inspired by the real-life Inspector Jonathan Whicher, best known today for his investigation of the Road Hill murder, memorably recounted by Kate Summerscale in *The Suspicions of Mr Whicher* (2008).

The introduction of the plainclothes detective in England slightly postdates a parallel development in France, where the Brigade de la Sûreté was founded in 1811 by Eugène Vidocq. Despite having got there first, the French language has subsequently adopted the English word as *détective*. In English, *detective* is shortened to the slang terms *tec* and *dick* (or *private dick*), which may in turn be lengthened as *Richard*, or *private Richard*. In mid-nineteenth-century America investigating officers were known as *Pinkertons*, or *Pinkerton detectives*, after Scotsman Allan Pinkerton, who set up an investigating bureau in Chicago in 1850. American detectives are also known as *gumshoes*, hinting at the way detectives operated by stealth. To act by *stealth* originally referred to a secret act of appropriation without permission—it is etymologically linked to *steal*; the word's modern use has preserved the association with clandestine or secretive behaviour, but lost its connections with pilfering. The US detective is also known as a *private eye*; while the image of an eye secretly observing is very apt for a detective, the term originated as a pun on the initial letter of *investigator*. *Investigator* is itself from Latin *vestigium* 'footprint' (also the root of *vestige* 'trace') referencing one method of tracking a potential criminal. The word *sleuth*, another nineteenth-century development in the lexicon of detection, was originally *sleuth-hound*, the term for a bloodhound with an acute sense of smell used for pursuing a *sleuth*—from the Old Norse word *sloð*, meaning 'track, trail'. The parallel between hunting villains and foxes lies behind Sherlock Holmes's famous exclamation *The game's afoot!*, as he rallies Watson to prepare for action. This phrase is a reduced form of *on foot*, and refers to the hunted animal being on its feet and prepared to run.

Also of hunting origin is the term *red herring*, a misleading clue, which originally described the way a cured herring takes on a red hue as a result of the smoking process. Smoked herring were employed to set a false hunting trail, tricking the hounds into following the scent, and thereby exercising the horses which pursued them. In the nineteenth century it was incorrectly assumed that the laying of red herring was a deliberate attempt to distract the hounds from the pursuit of the hunted animal, or *quarry*—originally the term for the parts of the butchered deer that were given to the hounds as a reward (from Anglo Norman *cuir* 'skin', because it was placed on the hide). This idea of a deliberate deception lies behind the use of the term in detective fiction as a false clue intentionally designed to mislead.

Nowadays detectives draw upon the latest advances in forensic sciences; this term derives from Latin *forum*—the name for the assembly place in Rome where public business, including judicial matters, was handled. But others rely on more traditional methods, such as an intuition or *hunch*—from a verb meaning to nudge someone in order to direct their attention. The great fictional detective Hercule Poirot was rather disdainful of such methods, preferring instead to rely on the workings of his *little grey cells*.

The methods of surveillance used by police detectives have much in common with those involved in the spy trade. Surveillance comes from the French *sur* 'over' and *veiller* 'to watch', itself from Latin *vigilare* 'to keep awake'. *Espionage*, the practice of governments using spies to obtain political or military secrets from their rivals, derives from Old French *espier* 'to spy', which is also the root of *spy* (modern French *espion*). The *clandestine* (from Latin *clam* 'secretly') nature of the job means that a number of vaguer euphemisms are commonly employed, such as *operative, agent, asset, intelligence officer*—even the term *secretary* has its origins in the spy trade, since it was originally used of a confidential agent, as its etymology implies (from Latin *secretum* 'secret'). Slang terms, however, can be more descriptive, such as *spook*, referencing the agent's shadowy existence, or *sleeper*, used of an undercover spy who has been inactive for a time. A *mole* is an operative who spends long periods working undercover—just as a mole burrows deep underground—achieving the trust and confidence of a state or organization, and passing on confidential information. In the seventeenth century, spies were also known as *flies*—a reference to their ability to gain access to private areas, pre-served in the expression *fly on the wall*. Since the 1930s, the job of listening to private conversations has been carried out by a con-cealed recording device known as a *bug*. A less high-tech method of overhearing a private conversation is to engage in *eavesdropping*. The origins of this term lie in the *eavesdrop*—originally *eaves drip*—an Old English word for the part of the ground surrounding a building where the rainwater that drips off the side of the building falls.

Unsurprisingly, a number of terms associated with espionage are of Russian extraction. An agent who runs a network of spies in a foreign country is known as a *resident*—a rendering of the Russian *rezident*, used in the same sense but originally referring to a member of the diplomatic service. *Disinformation*, the practice of deliberately spreading false information—also known as *black propaganda* and more recently *fake news*—is from Russian *dezinformacija*. Also of Russian origin is *Smersh*, the popular name of the Russian counter-espionage organization set up during the Second World War with responsibility for ensuring security within the Soviet intelligence service. Despite its rather comic-sounding name, its origins are rather more sinister—it is an abbreviation of Russian *smert' shpionam*, which means 'death to spies'. Its earliest appearance in English was in the first of Ian Fleming's James Bond novels, *Casino Royale* (1953).

Members of the British army are divided into various ranks indicative of their status. Within the officer category, these include *general* (originally *captain general*, from French *capitaine général* 'commander-in-chief'); *brigadier* (properly *brigadier general*—a general in charge of a *brigade*, from Italian *brigata* 'company'); *colonel*, going back to Latin *columna* 'column', referring to a commander in charge of a column of soldiers, while a *corporal* oversaw a body of soldiers (Latin *corpus*). A *lieutenant* is one who takes the place of another, or who acts on behalf of a superior, from French *lieu* 'place' and *tenant* 'holding', such as a *captain* (from Latin *caput* 'head'). An *adjutant*, the army term for an assisting officer, was originally used of a helper—it is from Latin *adjutans* 'being of service to'. *Sergeant*, a rank used by several of the forces, is from Latin *servire* 'to serve', originally used of an attendant or common soldier. The word *soldier* goes back to the Latin *solidus*, the name for a gold coin with which Roman soldiers were paid for their service.

The RAF ranks make use of the terms *commander*, 'one who commands', and *marshal*, originally the term for someone whose job was to look after horses, from Old English *mearh* 'horse' (as in *mare*) and *scealc* 'servant'. Since horses occupied a prominent role in medieval warfare, the term came to be used to refer to important positions in the royal household and the army. In the navy the chief rank is that of *admiral*, from Arabic *amir* 'commander'; the 'al' ending is a form of the definite article equivalent to *the*—in full the title was *amir-al-umara* 'ruler of rulers'. Also unique to the navy is the rank of *ensign*—from Latin *insignia* 'signs of office'; this was originally used of a badge of office or a banner, and then of the flag-bearer or soldier responsible for carrying the ensign. The origins of the rank of *midshipman* are rather more self-explanatory; it is quite simply a reference to the location on the ship where the officer was stationed.

The law

The word *law* is drawn from the Old Norse word *lagu*, the plural of *lag* 'something laid down or fixed', as in a market price, or the terms of a partnership. Surprisingly, this word is not thought to be related to Latin *lex* 'law', which is the source of *legal* and, via Old French *loial*, *loyal*. The Latin *lex* derives from the same root as *legere* 'to read, collect, gather', also the source of *legend* and *lecture*. Another Latin word for the law, *jus*, is the root of *just* and *justice*. *Judge* is also of Latin origin; it derives from Latin *judex*, the title for the person who decided a case in a court of law, which comprises *jus* 'law, right' and *dicus* 'speaking'. The Old English word for a law or judgement was *dom*—the root of modern English *doom*, which is etymologically related to the verb *to do*. Today *doom* is associated with condemning someone to death and destruction; it is also preserved in *Doomsday*— the Old English name for the Christian concept of the Last Judgement. A judgement that is particularly severe may be described as *draconian*. This is a reference to a Greek lawmaker of the seventh century BC named Draco, whose laws were famous for their harshness.

A *barrister* was originally known as a *barrister-at-law*; the name is a reference to the bar at which they stand (from Latin *barra*), and modelled on nouns like *chorister* and *minister*. The same root (via Italian *barista*) gives us *barista*, originally a bartender, but more commonly now someone who works in a coffee shop. In Scotland, the equivalent title for a person who supports another in a legal case is *advocate*, from Latin *advocatus* (itself from *advocare* 'to summon'). A devil's advocate, originally someone pleading an evil cause, now refers to a person deliberately adopting a contentious viewpoint in order to provoke discussion or to test a particular theory. Although its origins lie in the Nahuatl (a language spoken by the Aztecs in Mexico) word *ahuacatl*, the word *avocado* has been influenced by the Spanish word for an advocate, following confusion concerning the two words in the seventeenth century. Although Spanish now uses *aguacate* for the avocado pear, in French *avocat* refers to both the fruit and the lawyer. Uncertainty over this newfangled term in seventeenth-century England prompted the reinterpretation of *avocado* as *alligator pear*. Other terms for legal representatives are *attorney* (from Old French *atorner* 'to assign'), and *solicitor* (from Latin *sollicitus* 'anxious'). A *notary*, or *notary public*, who is licensed to draw up contracts, was originally a clerk or secretary, from Latin *notarius*—derived from *nota* 'mark'.

In the courtroom, the accused is made to stand in the *dock*. Originally designed to hold all the various criminals who were due to stand trial on a particular day, the word probably derives from the Flemish *dok*, designating a 'chicken coop'. The *jury* takes its name from Latin *jurare* 'to swear'; someone who swears an oath in court that they know to be untrue has committed *perjury*, from Latin *perjurium* 'false oath'. Both *testify* and *testimony* go back to Latin *testis* 'witness'—the same word may lie behind *testicles*, which get their name from the idea that they testify to a man's virility. A meeting convened for judicial purposes in Anglo-Saxon England was known as a *moot*. This word survives today as the name given to a mock trial at which university law students learn the skills of debating and trying invented cases. Because issues discussed at a moot were frequently open to debate and difficult to resolve, this gave rise to the phrase *moot point*—referring to any issue that is similarly open to discussion. The association of the moot today with debating hypothetical cases for purely academic purposes has led to the additional sense of 'abstract, irrelevant'—now the main sense in the US. If a hearing is *adjourned*, it is stopped in order to be resumed at a later date. Its original sense, however, was a summons to appear in court on a particular day; this meaning is reflected in its etymology—it is from Old French *ajorner*, literally 'to a day'. The Greek word for an eyewitness, *autoptes*, literally 'seen by self', is the origin of *autopsy*—an investigation into the cause of a person's death.

It's clear from this discussion that the language of the law is heavily indebted to Latin; indeed, many legal phrases used today remain entirely in Latin. A lawyer who works on a case *pro bono* has waived the right to charge a fee; this phrase is a contracted form of the Latin *pro bono publico* 'for the public good'. A writ that requires attendance in court to answer a charge is known as a *subpoena*; failure to appear will incur a penalty. Meaning 'under penalty', the *subpoena* takes its name from the opening words of a Latin writ issued by the Court of Chancery in the fifteenth century, requiring a defendant to appear in court to answer a charge; non-attendance would incur a penalty. *Affidavit*, a written statement confirmed by oath that is used as evidence in a court, is the third person singular past tense form of the Latin verb *affidare*; the word literally means 'he has stated on oath'.

Some legal terms have lost their technical sense and entered the language more generally. An *apology* was initially a legal term for a speech given in defence of a person in response to a specific charge (from Greek *apo* 'away' and *logia* 'speaking'). In subsequent developments it was used non-technically to describe an explanation, and then one that was accompanied by an expression of regret for any offence caused. Also originating in legal parlance is *ignoramus*; from a Latin word meaning 'we do not know', this word was initially a verdict made by a jury when confronted with insufficient evidence. Today an *innuendo* is a sly remark or hint, but its origins lie in the glossing of legal documents. Its original Latin meaning is 'by nodding at', from *in* 'towards' and *nuere* 'to nod'; it was added to legal documents in the sense 'that is to say', as an introduction to an explanation or gloss. A similar development may be seen in the verb *insinuate*. This word is now used to refer to an oblique hint or suggestion, but originally referred to the process of entering a record into a legal register. *Paraphernalia* is now used of a collection of miscellaneous objects; its origins, however, lie in a legal term referring to the property owned by a woman that was not transferred to her husband on marriage—it derives from the Greek term *parapherna*, meaning 'property apart from a dowry'.

Other examples are words that have preserved their legal sense, but have developed a looser, non-technical meaning. For example, in court a defendant may offer an *alibi*—evidence showing that, at the time an offence was committed, the person concerned was somewhere else and so could not have been the perpetrator. This is a borrowing of the Latin *alibi* 'elsewhere', a form of *alius* 'another' (also the root of *alien*); the word has been used in this legal sense since the eighteenth century, but more recently it has developed the looser sense of 'excuse' or 'pretext'.

Crime

The words *crime* and *criminal* go back to Latin *crimen* 'charge, accusation', ultimately deriving from a base related to *cernere* 'to separate, decide', or more technically in legal usage 'to make known a determination'—also found in *discern*. *Felony* was originally the term used for a more serious crime; it originates in an Old French word meaning 'wicked', which is the source of the word *fell* 'cruel', preserved in the phrase *one fell swoop*—originally a quotation from *Macbeth*—often mistakenly reinterpreted today as *one foul swoop*. More minor crimes were known as *misdemeanours*, which literally means 'bad behaviour'. Although it is now used of a criminal attack on a person, the term *assault* originates in a Latin word meaning 'leap upon', from *ad* 'towards' and *salire* 'to leap'. In legal parlance *assault* can be used to refer to the threat of such an attack, while the word *battery* (from French *battre* 'to beat') is added when the physical threat has been carried out. *Affray*, a legal term describing a disturbance of the peace, originally referred to the state of being alarmed or frightened, and is from the same root as *afraid*.

Blackmail, the practice of demanding money in exchange for silence, goes back to a sixteenth-century tribute demanded by Scottish chiefs from farmers in return for protection. The term itself derives from the obsolete *mail*, 'rent, tribute', borrowed from Old Norse. The idea of *black* mail may have been influenced by the existence of *white rent*, a duty that was paid by a freeholder in lieu of services; here the use of the colour term is probably the result of confusion over the term *quit-rent*. *Arson*—deliberately setting fire to someone else's property—goes back to the Latin *ardere* 'to burn'—also the source of *ardent*, literally 'burning', but now used metaphorically to mean 'extremely keen'. *Embezzlement*, the term used in corporate fraud for misappropriating money that belongs to an organization, is from the Anglo-Norman *enbesiler* 'to make off with', which is related to Old French *besillier* 'ravage'. *Forgery* derives from the use of the verb *to forge*, meaning 'fashion, construct'—itself descended from the Latin *fabricare*, the origin of *fabricate* 'to make something with skill', now more commonly used to mean 'to invent something in order to deceive'. *Libel* and *slander* are both terms that refer to making false statements that damage the reputation of another person. The key difference being that, whereas slander (a variant form of *scandal*—from Latin *scandalum* 'cause of offence') is a spoken statement, libel is used to refer to a claim that has been published—reflecting its origins in Latin *libellus*, the diminutive form of *liber* 'book'.

CHAPTER 7

Politics

Politics has its roots in Aristotle's treatise on statecraft titled *Ta Politika*, referring to affairs that concern the public—its origins lie in the Greek word *polis* 'city, state' (as in *metropolis*). *Democracy*, a system of government where the people play a part—typically by voting for their elected representatives—is from the Greek *demos* 'people' and *kratia* 'power'. The word *aristocracy* originally referred to a form of government consisting of those considered to be the state's best citizens—from Greek *aristos* 'best'. It later came to signal those members of a society who were the most wealthy and of the most exalted birth, leading to its modern meaning, 'nobility'. Numerous parallel terms have been coined using this formation, reflecting a range of approaches to government—encompassing *meritocracy* (government by those chosen on merit), *plutocracy* (where power is accorded to the richest people—from Greek *ploutos* 'wealth'), and even *kleptocracy*, government by thieves (from Greek *kleptes* 'thief'—as in *kleptomania*).

The word *government* is from Latin *gubernare* 'to steer', originally referring to someone who steers a ship. The word is ultimately based on Greek *kubernetes* 'steersman', the source of the twentieth-century formation *cybernetics*. *Parliament* is from French *parler* 'to talk', reflecting its function as a place for debate and discussion, or—more cynically—a talking shop. The same origin lies behind *parlour*, which was originally the name for a room in a monastery set aside for meeting and discoursing with guests. French *parler* has its roots in the Latin *parabola* 'comparison', which is also the origin of *parable*—a story with a moral message—ultimately from a Greek word meaning 'place alongside'. The *cabinet*, formed of the senior ministers responsible for deciding policy, gets its name from the private chamber in which it meets; the word literally means 'little cabin'. A similar origin lies behind Cobra—the title given to the emergency meetings convened at times of national crisis. Despite its *sinister*-sounding name (*sinister* from a Latin word meaning 'left hand'), its origins are disappointingly practical—Cobra stands for Cabinet Office Briefing Room A. The *exchequer* is etymologically connected to the word *chess* (via medieval Latin *scaccus* 'check'), since the Norman administrators practised their accounting using counters on a chequered board, known as an exchequer.

Elections

The word *campaigning* draws upon a term first used in a military context; it originates in Latin *campania* 'open countryside', and referred to the practice of an army moving from a fortress to the open field during the summer months. Those submitting to the process are termed *candidates*, from the Latin *candidus* 'white', since one who aspired to public office was expected to wear a white toga to reflect their spotless character. In order to win an election, candidates engage in *canvassing*, a metaphorical use that reflects the way that discussing an issue was likened to tossing something in a canvas sheet. Candidates travelling extensively in an effort to build support for their campaign are the source of the word *ambitious*, which is from Latin *ambire* 'to go about'. *Hustings*, public forums at which candidates set out their policies and answer questions from the electorate, is from the Old Norse *husthing*—the term for a household assembly. *Husthing* is a compound of *hus* 'house' and *thing*, the Norse word for a parliament, still used in the name of the Icelandic National

Parliament, the Alþingi. The word *vote* originates in the Latin *votum* 'vow, offering, prayer'; an alternative Latin term was *suffragium*, from which we get *suffrage* and *suffragette*. The process of voting involves placing a tick on a ballot paper; *ballot* is from Italian *ballotta* 'little ball', and refers to an earlier practice of registering a vote by dropping coloured balls into a container. This method of casting a vote lies behind the phrase *blackball*, referring to the rejection of a candidate for membership of some exclusive establishment by placing a black ball into the box. The study of elections and voting is known as *psephology*, from Greek *psephos* 'pebble', referencing a similar practice of using small stones to cast votes. Predictions of outcomes draw upon *exit polls*; from a Germanic word meaning 'head', a poll came to refer to the number of people determined by counting heads—from which the sense of the number of votes cast emerged.

CHAPTER 8

The Church

The word *church* is one of a handful of borrowings into Old English from Greek, in this instance from *kuriakon* 'of the lord', referring originally to one who had authority over a household. The Christians employed this word to refer to their lord Jesus Christ, and coined the term *kuriakon doma* 'Lord's house', from which we get the English word *church*. Another term for a church derives from Greek *ekklesia* (from a root meaning 'call out'), the root of *ecclesiastical*; this word was used by the Greeks to refer to an assembly at which adult Athenian males made decisions about the running of the city. Although it is now a noun referring to the building in which a bishop and his staff administer the diocese, *cathedral* was formerly an adjective used to describe a church containing a bishop's throne (from Greek *kathedra* 'seat'). The *bishop* who occupies the seat is also from Greek; Old English *biscop* represents one of the earliest such borrowings (from *episkopos* 'overseer', a title used of one supervising the work of builders or slaves). The district over which a bishop has jurisdiction is termed a *diocese*, a word drawn from the Greek *dioikesis* 'administration', from *dioikein* 'to keep house'—the term employed by the emperor Diocletian when he divided up the empire into twelve districts.

Below the bishop in the ecclesiastical hierarchy is the *priest*, a title that is ultimately based upon Latin *presbyter* 'elder'. Latin also employed *sacerdos*, from *sacer* 'holy', which gives us the English words *sacred, sacrifice,* and *sacrilege,* literally 'robber of holy things'. The traditional parish church is overseen by a *vicar,* taking its name from Latin *vicarius* 'proxy' (also the root of *vicarious,* referring to something done on behalf of another), this word originally referred to the vicar's position as substitute for the true parson or rector, drawing upon its earlier use for the individual appointed to oversee a diocese in the Roman empire. Below the vicar is the *curate,* from Latin *cura* 'care', this term was initially employed of any minister of the church with *pastoral* (from Latin *pastor* 'shepherd') responsibility, but is now specifically accorded to a trainee or assistant member of the *clergy* (from Latin *clericus* 'clergyman'). A role that did not require the administration of pastoral care was known as a *sinecure* (Latin *sine* 'without' and *cura* 'care')—now used of any job that confers status and financial benefits but involves little actual work. The lowly status of the curate in relation to the lofty bishop is apparent in the origins of the phrase *curate's egg* to refer to something of mixed standards. It developed from a cartoon entitled 'True Humility' that appeared in *Punch* magazine in 1895, in which a curate, finding himself served with a bad egg when dining at the bishop's table, reassures his host that 'parts of it are excellent'.

Exclusive to the Roman Catholic (Greek *katholikos* 'universal') Church is the role of the *cardinal,* a member of the pope's council. The name is a metaphorical use of the Latin *cardo* 'hinge', literally meaning 'pertaining to a hinge', and thus 'chief, principal'. The same image lies behind the use of the word in the *cardinal virtues* (justice, prudence, temperance, and fortitude), the *cardinal points* (north, south, east, and west), and the *cardinal numbers: one, two, three* (as opposed to the *ordinal numbers: first, second, third*). *Pontiff,* an alternative title for the pope, is from Latin *pontifex,* literally 'bridge-builder'. Someone who takes on the role of the pontiff in officiating at a Mass is said to *pontificate*—from this we get the more common modern usage 'express views in a dogmatic manner'. The pope himself gets his title from the Greek *papas* 'bishop', a variant form of *pappas* 'father'. The Italian word for father, *padre*, is also used as a title for a priest in various countries and denominations; in the UK it is particularly associated with the armed forces, where it is employed alongside the term *chaplain*. *Chaplain*, and the related word *chapel*, are from Latin *cappella* 'little cloak', which originally referred to the officials (*cappellani*) who were tasked with taking custody of the cloak of St Martin by the Frankish kings, who had the relic carried before them in battle. From this specific use, the word's remit was broadened to encompass any sanctuary containing holy relics, and then any place of worship distinct from a church. An earlier name for a sacred building of this kind was Latin *oratorium* 'place of prayer', from which *oratory* is derived. The church building consists of a *nave*—the central section in which the congregation is seated—from Latin *navis* 'ship', a reference to the way the ceiling above the nave resembles an inverted ship's hull. The section of the church near to the altar reserved for the clergy, separated from the main church by steps or a *rood* screen (from Old English *rod* 'cross'), is known as the *chancel* (from Latin *cancelli* 'crossbars'—a reference to a lattice screen that separated the altar from the nave). The word *chancel* is connected to *chancellor*, from Latin *cancellarius*, the term for a court official who was seated behind a grating. There is a further connection with *cancel*, since this verb describes the process of expunging using a series of crossed lines, or *crossing out*. The *aisle*, now used of the passages between rows of seats in theatres, cinemas, and trains, is from Latin *ala* 'wing'; the spelling of the English word shows the influence of the French form, *aile*, as well as confusion with *isle*.

A Jewish temple is known as a *synagogue*, from a Greek word meaning 'meeting', from *sun* 'together' and *agein* 'to bring'. *Mosque* was introduced into English in the sixteenth century from French, having been borrowed into French from Italian. Its ultimate origin is the Arabic word for the place of worship and prayer, *masjid*, which is derived from the verb *sajada*, meaning 'bow down in prayer'. *Islam*, the name for the Muslim religion, is derived from an Arabic word meaning 'submission'—specifically submission to the will of God. This word goes back to the verb *salima*, 'to become secure', which is also the origin of *Muslim* and of *salaam*, meaning 'peace' (also found in the Hebrew word *shalom*). The Muslim holy scriptures are known as the *Koran* or *Quran*, transliterations of an Arabic word meaning 'recitation', related to a verb meaning 'read'.

CHAPTER 9

Health services

This section will examine the various terms used of and by those working in the caring professions—often a source of some confusion for patients, especially ones with 'small Latin and less Greek' (as Ben Jonson described Shakespeare). An important root is the Latin *hospis*—the source of a variety of English words describing people or places where one can find support or sanctuary: *hospital, host, hostel, hotel, hospice*. Given these associations, it is surprising to find that *hospis* is also the root of *hostile*, via the related word *hostis* 'enemy'. The word *clinic* is from the Greek word *kline* meaning 'bed' (from a stem meaning 'lie back'—also preserved in *recline* and *decline*); clinical medicine originated in the phrase *klinike tekhne* 'bedside art', referring to the way it was taught at the bedside.

Nurse is from Latin *nutrix*, from *nutrire* 'to nourish'; from this same root we get the words *nutrient* and *nutritious*. *Doctor* derives from the Latin verb *docere* 'to teach', reflecting the word's origins in the term for an advanced scholar or university teacher—as in the title *Doctor of Philosophy*. *Surgeon* comes from Greek *kheirourgia* (via Latin *chirurgia*) and refers to the practice of working with one's hands (from Greek *kheir* 'hand'), as distinct from other kinds of doctor who administer medicines. *Chirurgeon* was used as an alternative to *surgeon* in English up to the nineteenth century; it survives today in the abbreviation MBChB used of a medical degree.

The Greek term for a doctor was *iatros*, which is preserved as the second element of labels for particular branches of medicine, such as *geriatrics* (Greek *geras* 'old age') and *paediatrics*—the branch of medicine that specializes in children's care (from Greek *pais* 'boy, child'). The Greek word *pais* is from the same root as Latin *puer* 'boy', the source of *puerile*—originally a purely descriptive term designating something that was characteristic or suitable for a boy or child, now used in a derogatory sense to mean 'childish, infantile', or just plain silly. The *paed-* element is also found in *orthopaedics*—now a branch of medicine that is concerned with resolving problems with the musculoskeletal system generally, but originally confined specifically to correcting bone deformities in children. The *ortho-* element is from the Greek word *orthos*, meaning 'straight, correct'—also found in *orthodontics*, the field of dentistry concerned with correcting irregularities in the teeth and jaw. Paediatrics should not be confused with *podiatry*, from Greek *pous* 'foot', the branch of medicine that is concerned with feet—a mistake made by Basil Fawlty in the BBC sitcom *Fawlty Towers*. When corrected, Basil defended his misapprehension with the memorable: 'Well, children have feet don't they?' An alternative term for a podiatrist is *chiropodist*, a combination of the Greek words for hand and foot formed in the late eighteenth century, and now used specifically of someone who treats bunions and corns.

The word *patient* is from Latin *patiens* 'able to stand up to, undergo', from the verb *pati* 'to suffer'. Patients present their *symptoms* (from a Greek word referring to a chance occurrence), from which doctors offer a *diagnosis*. The word *diagnosis* is a seventeenth-century formulation using the Greek *gignoskein* 'to discern, perceive'; based upon their assessment the doctor will make a *prognosis*—a forecast of the likely progression of the disease (from *pro* 'in advance' and *gignoskein*). The doctor may decide to *prescribe* (from Latin *praescribere* 'to direct in writing') a treatment, or a course of action—usually eat more fruit and veg, drink less, and take more exercise. In an ideal scenario, the doctor may be in a position to offer a *panacea*, a remedy for every type of illness, from *pan* 'all' and *akos* 'remedy'—the name given by the Greeks to a plant thought to be able to cure all diseases, also personified as the daughter of Asclepius, the god of healing. Alternatively, the patient may have to settle for a *placebo*, from the Latin verb *placere* 'to please', and meaning 'I shall be pleasing'. In the Middle Ages the expression to *sing placebo* meant to flatter or act the sycophant; today a placebo is a drug that is given to a patient more for the psychological benefit than for any therapeutic effects, or a drug with no benefits that is prescribed as a control in a test for a new treatment.

If the condition requires more specialist treatment, the patient will be referred to the relevant hospital department; this is where things get linguistically more challenging, since the terms for medical specialisms generally draw upon little-known Greek and Latin roots. A referral to *cardiology* is fairly straightforward, since most people are familiar with the Greek word *kardia* 'heart', thanks to the phrase *cardiac arrest*—a cessation, or *arrest*, of the heart's pumping action. The Latin form of this word, *cor*, is perhaps less familiar, although it does appear in *cordial*—originally a drink thought to stimulate the heart. But while *cardiology* may be widely understood, terms like *haematology* (from Greek *haima* 'blood'), *ophthalmology* (from Greek *ophthalmos* 'eye'), and *gynaecology* (from Greek *gune* 'woman') are more *opaque* (from Latin *opacus* 'darkened'). What is it about the English language that using transparent labels like 'Eye department' or 'Women's medicine' would feel like cheating?

Gastroenterology (from Greek *gaster* 'stomach') presents particular challenges since it is easily confused with *gastronomy*, the art and science of fine dining. *Nephrology* is the area of medicine that deals with the kidneys, from Greek *nephros* 'kidney'. The Latin for kidneys, *renes*, is the source of the adjective *renal*—found in medical terms like *renal artery* and *renal dialysis*. *Urology* draws upon the Greek *ouron* 'urine'; it is a nineteenth-century coinage, when the equivalent—and more easily understood—form *urinology* (from Latin *urina*) was also in use. *Oncology* is from Greek *onkos* 'mass, bulk', used in Byzantine Greek to mean 'tumour'—the origin of its modern usage, since oncology is the science and treatment of tumours. Such tumours may be a sign of *cancer* (from the Latin word for a crab—so called because a cancerous tumour was thought to resemble a crab), or may be *benign*—from Latin *bene* 'well' and *genus* 'born'.

Modern treatments have come a long way since the Middle Ages, but the key terms of medieval medicine are still in use today—albeit with different senses. During the medieval period it was believed that a person's health was ruled by four fluids, known as *humours* (from Latin *humor* 'liquid, moisture'). From this, *humour* came to be used in the sense 'state of mind, mood', and then 'inclination, fancy'. The word subsequently began to refer to strange or fanciful behaviour, from which the modern sense of comical, or being able to appreciate something comical, arose. Maintaining a balance of these humours was crucial to a healthy life; the word *temperament*, from Latin *tempero* 'I mix', refers to the way that the blend of these humours was considered to be central to a person's disposition. When the mixture is upset, or in incorrect proportions, this creates a *distemper*—originally used of any illness, but now limited to a disease found in animals, especially dogs. An excess of one or more of the humours was known as a *plethora*, from a Greek word meaning 'fullness'—subsequently used of any overabundance but now more neutrally to refer to a large quantity. The humours were also thought to influence a person's outward appearance, especially that of the face; from this we get the modern use of *complexion*, which—like *temperament*—was originally used of the relative proportions of the humours—from Latin *complectere* 'to plait together'. Bad temper was thought to be stored in the spleen, an abdominal organ responsible for producing and removing blood cells, which gave rise to the expression *vent one's spleen*, meaning 'express feelings of anger'.

The four humours were blood, melancholy, choler, and phlegm. *Choler* is from the Greek *khole* 'bile', an excess of which was supposed to cause irritability and anger—the source of modern English *choleric* 'bad tempered, irascible' (from Latin *irasci* 'to grow angry', from *ira* 'anger'). *Melancholy* is black bile, from Greek *melan* 'black' (also the root of *melanoma*); an excess of this fluid was thought to be the cause of depression—the source of the modern meaning 'sadness, dejection'. Someone suffering from an excess of blood was *sanguine* (from Latin *sanguis* 'blood')—characterized by a red face and an optimistic outlook. This is the origin of the modern use of *sanguine* to refer to a positive approach to a difficult situation. *Phlegm* is from a Latin word signifying 'clammy', itself from a Greek verb meaning 'burn, blaze'; someone suffering from an excess of this humour was thought to be lazy and apathetic. The word has since taken on something of a positive development, as it now describes a phlegmatic person with a propensity to remain calm when under pressure.

While our medical understanding may have advanced considerably, some medical terms preserve long-superseded theories about illness. *Malaria*, for instance, gets its name from the Italian *mala aria* 'bad air', since it was believed to have been caused by the poor air quality of the marshlands in some districts of Italy, and other hot countries. In fact the disease was carried by mosquitoes, known to the Greeks as *konops*, from which we get *canopy*—originally a net offering protection against the insects. Although it is no longer thought to be a disease of the womb suffered only by women, the disturbance of the nervous system known as *hysteria* preserves its etymological link with this supposed cause (from Greek *hustera* 'womb'). *Flu* is a shortening of *influenza*, the Italian form of *influence* (from Latin *influere* 'to flow in')—a word which referred specifically to the medieval belief that a person's life and fortune were influenced by an ethereal fluid that flowed from the stars. The image of flowing and dripping is central to the names by which a number of diseases are known. The sexually transmitted disease *gonorrhoea* gets its name from Greek *gonos* 'seed' and *rhoia* 'flux, flow'—an element also found in *haemorrhoids* 'flowing of blood' and *catarrh* 'flowing down'. *Diarrhoea* 'flowing through' nicely captures this particular complaint, without being too specific about what exactly is flowing through where. This condition is also known as *dysentery*, which literally means 'bad bowels'. Similarly, *diabetes* is from the Greek word for a siphon, going back to the verb *diabainein* 'to go through', referring to the tendency for sufferers to be regularly passing water. *Gout* is from Latin *gutta* 'drop', because it was thought to be caused by corrupt blood dripping into a joint. Other names are drawn from the manner in which the disease manifests itself; *shingles*, an inflammation that typically results in a rash around the middle of the body, takes its name from the Latin *cingulum* 'girdle'. *Nausea*, now a general term for a feeling of sickness, originally referred more specifically to the inclination to vomit induced by sea travel—it is from Greek *naus* 'ship', also the root of *nautical*.

Nowadays it is possible to treat many of the commonest infectious diseases with antibiotics, such as *penicillin*, from Latin *penicillus*, literally 'small tail'—also used of a paintbrush because of its similar appearance (and the origin of *pencil*). The antibiotic was given this name because the hairs on the mould cells resemble small paintbrushes. Alternatively, some conditions may be prevented entirely using *inoculation*—originally a horticultural term for the grafting of a bud from one plant into another. The word for a bud was *oculus*, also the term for the eye—found in *binoculars*, which literally means 'having two eyes'. Medical treatments are more usually administered by tablet or by *syringe*—from *syrinx*, the name of the pan pipes. This name is derived from that of a nymph who was pursued by the god Pan; in order to protect her chastity she was changed into reeds by the water nymphs. Pan used the reeds to construct a pipe and named it after Syrinx. *Vaccines* (from Latin *vacca* 'cow') are so called because of Edward Jenner's discovery that contact with cowpox (a milder form of smallpox) resulted in milkmaids becoming immune to smallpox.

Dentistry

The word *dentist* is from Latin *dens* 'tooth', or rather from the inflected form *dentem*; in the sixteenth century toothpaste was known by the French word *dentifrice*, a compound of *dentem* and *fricare* 'to rub'. Despite their differences, the Old English word *top* and the Latin *dens* are from the same root; this is also the source of the Greek word *odous*, from which the less common adjective *odontic* 'relating to the teeth' is derived.

The front teeth are known as the *incisors*, a Latin word meaning 'cutter', from the verb *incidere* 'to cut'. Behind these are the four *canines*, which take their name from the Latin word *canis* 'dog'. Where the incisors and canines are primarily employed for tearing, the teeth behind these, known as *molars*, are used for chewing and grinding—from Latin *molaris* 'grinding tooth', the adjective related to *mola* 'millstone'. Behind these are the *wisdom teeth*; this name is based upon similar names found in Arabic and ancient Greek, and refers to the way that these teeth do not erupt (that is, break through the gum into the mouth) until the age of around 20, considered to be the age one also acquires wisdom. These teeth may also be distinguished according to whether they appear in the upper, or *maxillary* (from Latin *maxilla* 'jaw'), jaw or the lower, or *mandibular* (from Latin *mandere* 'to chew'), jaw.

Hairdressing

It might seem odd to include hairdressers alongside doctors and dentists, but in the Middle Ages all three trades were practised by one individual, known as a *barber-surgeon*. In the fifteenth century barbers and surgeons were separated, and only barbers were permitted to carry out dentistry; it was not until the eighteenth century that two separate corporations of barbers and surgeons were officially formulated. *Barber* is from the Latin *barba* 'beard'; the same word lies behind *rebarbative* 'repellent, objectionable', which literally means 'standing against each other beard to beard'. The idea that standing face to face with someone is an act of aggression is also preserved in *confront*, meaning 'stand face to face'—from Latin *frons* 'face'. Likewise, an *affront* is an insult that is directed *ad frontem*—to the face. For a more defiant gesture of opposition, you could choose to *take one by the beard*, *make one's beard*, or—if you're feeling especially brave—*beard the lion in his den*.

Alternative terms for a barber include *hairdresser* (from the verb *dress*, meaning 'to set in order, prepare'), *hair stylist*, as well as others, like *tonsorialist* (from Latin *tonsor* 'barber') and *trichotomist* (from a Greek verb meaning 'to cut the hair') that are now obsolete. Thankfully, the tradition of barbers leaving musical instruments for their customers to play while waiting to be served has also fallen out of favour. This practice is the source of the term *barber's music*, used to refer to any kind of musical *cacophony* (Greek *kakos* 'bad' and *phone* 'sound'), as recorded in Pepys's Diary: 'My Lord called for the Lieutenant's Gitterne, and with two Candlesticks with money in them for Symballs we made...barber's Musique.'

The name given to the distinctive *mullet* hairstyle, in which the hair is short at the front and sides but long at the back, is of disputed origins. One suggestion is that it is a contracted form of *mullet-head*, an American slang term for an idiot, in which *mullet* is from the fish of that name. The origins are discussed by the Beastie Boys, an American hip-hop band popular in the 1990s, in the lyrics of their song *Mullet Head*. A haircut that results in the hair being cut very short all over is known as a *buzz cut*. The origins of *quiff* are also uncertain; it may be related to the French verb *coiffer*, which is the root of *coiffure*, a fancy term for a hairstyle, and *coiffeur*, the French word for a hairdresser. Since the 1950s, *quiff* has referred to a hairstyle in which the hair is brushed upwards from the forehead (think of Morrissey or Tintin); however, it originally described a curl of hair that was stuck down on the forehead, a style of hair particularly associated with soldiers from the late nineteenth to the early twentieth centuries. *Sideburns* were originally *burnsides*, named after US General Ambrose E. Burnside (1824–81), who sported a particularly fine pair of side-whiskers (also known as *sideboards*). After the connection with the general was lost, the word was altered—presumably to emphasize the *side* element in an attempt to make sense of the word's meaning. Someone who lacked hair was known to the Anglo-Saxons as *calu*—the origin of our word *callow*. The connection isn't immediately obvious, since bald people are not necessarily weak and puny, while *callow* tends to be used of young people. But in fact the connection lies in a different use of the word *callow* to refer to featherless birds, and subsequently to the fluffy down of those birds that have not yet fledged, which was thought to resemble the downy chins of *pubescent* (reaching puberty, or adult-hood—from Latin *puber* 'adult') boys—what is today called *bum fluff*. The idea that hair is an index of authority and rank also surfaces in *bigwig*, a general term for someone of social significance, originating in the flowing wigs worn by important people and still sported by judges today.

CHAPTER 10

Parenting

It may be that your work is in the home, doing the household *chores*—this word is from Old English *cyrr* 'turn', and literally means a turn or stroke of work. The same word lies behind the old-fashioned *charwoman* for someone employed to help with the cleaning in an office or home. Another dated term, *batman*, now used of an army officer's personal servant or the caped crusader who watches over Gotham City, draws on the French *bât* 'packsaddle', referring to its earlier use of an orderly charged with looking after the officer's pack-horse. If you have children, your morning may be spent helping them get ready for school, or perhaps you have literally been left *holding the baby*—an expression that refers to being left with an unwelcome responsibility. If that phrase seems unduly harsh towards babies, they can at least take some comfort from the phrase *throw the baby out with the bathwater*, which refers to the danger of discarding something important along with something trivial. The word *baby* probably derives from the repetition of 'ba' sounds that an *infant* (from a Latin word meaning 'unable to speak') uses to communicate; a similar origin also lies behind the names *mama* and *papa*. *Babble*, a term used to describe incoherent nonsense, is likely from the same source. Its adoption was probably encouraged by the similarity to the name of the Tower of Babel, which, according to the Bible story, was intended to reach heaven and was the reason God confounded human languages, thereby hindering human communication.

The medical care of women during pregnancy and childbirth is known as *obstetrics*; it originates in the Latin word *obstetrix* 'midwife'. From the Latin *obstare* 'stand in the way of', this term referred to the way a midwife shielded the woman from others during childbirth. The term *obstetrix* was used up to the late nineteenth century but was replaced by *midwife*; this word derives from Old English *mid* 'with' and *wife* 'woman'—its sense seems originally to have been 'woman who accompanies the mother at childbirth'. Since the role is sometimes filled by male practitioners, the term *male midwife* has been introduced, although an equivalent term, *man-midwife* (used initially to describe a midwife's male assistant), has been in use since the seventeenth century—as in the notorious Dr Slop of Laurence Sterne's novel *Tristram Shandy* (1759–67). *Maternity* is now widely used to refer to care surrounding childbirth; although *ante-* 'before', *post-* 'after', and *neo-* 'new' *natal* (from Latin *natalis* 'belonging to birth') are the usual terms.

The *caesarean section* is so called because Julius Caesar is said to have been delivered using this method. The *section* part comes from Latin *sectionem* 'cutting' (from *secare* 'to cut'); the more usual sense of *section*, 'distinct part or group', refers to a part that has been cut off, or separated, from the rest. The *elective section*, where a caesarean is the result of personal choice rather than medical necessity, is sometimes known by the disparaging term *too posh to push*.

The recent parental craze for uploading numerous photos of one's little darlings to social media has given rise to the term *sharenting*. *Helicopter parenting* captures the way overly protective parents hover over their offspring, patrolling their every move. The popularity of online discussion forums like Mumsnet has led to the coining of abbreviations for commonly discussed issues, such as the different theories of how to deal with a fractious child, including *AP* 'attachment parenting' versus *CIO* 'cry it out'. Also popular are blend formations like *lactivism*—the promotion of the benefits of breast- over bottle-feeding—and a whole load of *poo*-related formations, from *poomageddon* to *apoocalypse*.

As these terms suggest, looking after a baby involves a fair amount of time changing *nappies*. Nappies were originally square pieces of cloth folded into shape, rather than the made-to-fit disposable types used today. The name is an abbreviation of *napkin*, itself a diminutive form of Old French *nape* 'tablecloth', ultimately from Latin *mappa* 'map'. The US equivalent, *diaper*, gets its name from the fabric from which it was originally made. Ironically, given its use today, the word originates in medieval Greek *dia* 'across' and *aspros* 'white'— appropriate for a diaper in its clean state at least. The term for a newborn baby's first bowel movement—one of many words that you learn once you become a parent and never use again—is *meconium*. It originates in the Greek word *mekonion*, the name for the poppy, because the greenish-brown colour was thought to resemble the juice of the poppy; the same word lies behind the name of the pain-relieving drug *codeine* (from Greek *kodeia* 'poppy head').

If you are brave enough to consider leaving the house, you will need a *buggy, stroller*, or an old-fashioned *pram*. *Pram* is a shortened form of *perambulator*, a seventeenth-century term for a pedestrian, from Latin *perambulare* 'to walk about in, travel around in'. The word began life as a technical term to refer to a formal procession around the limits of a piece of land belonging to a manor or a parish—a process also known as *beating the bounds*, in reference to the practice of striking certain boundary markers with rods. This procedure originated in the Anglo-Saxon period when detailed maps were not readily available; marking the boundaries in this way was a useful means of checking and setting out the limits of a parish, while simultaneously observing the tradition of praying for the crops and a fruitful harvest. The root verb is *ambulare* 'to walk', which is also the source of *ambulance*—from French *hôpital ambulant* 'mobile hospital', since the earliest ambulances were drawn by horses so as to be able to follow troops during military campaigns.

But it may be that the days of *poonamis* and *toddler tantrums* are behind you; your little ones are now old enough to go to school. Or perhaps you yourself are a student or *scholar*—originally the term for someone who attends a school. *School* is from the ancient Greek word *skhole*, which referred to a learned disputation or lecture. It was also the Greek term for leisure, since having time to spend in education was a luxury enjoyed by the rich. The children of the less fortunate would have found themselves heading straight to the fields, or some other area of gainful employment. A similar connection is apparent in the Latin word for an elementary school, *ludus*, which also meant 'play, sport'—the root of *ludicrous*. Despite their name, English *public schools* (from Latin *publicus* 'belonging to the people, for everyone') are in fact highly exclusive fee-paying institutions. These are usually *boarding schools*—where pupils take their meals and accommodation in the school, only going home at the end of term. This use of *boarding* goes back to a Germanic word for a plank of wood, which was used to denote a table (as in *boardroom*) and then the meals served on it (as in *board and lodging*). Children are lodged in dormitories (from Latin *dormire* 'to sleep'), which are every bit as cold and spartan (after the inhabitants of Sparta, who famously shunned luxury) as the monastic bedrooms from which they take their name. It was in the public schools that the term *prefect*, or *præfect* as it was initially spelled, was first introduced to refer to a senior pupil given responsibility over juniors. This comes from Latin *praefectus*, a holder of a public office, or a governor of a province or city, from *prae* 'before' and *facere* 'to make, appoint'. *Prefect* is first recorded in the early nineteenth century; before that the correct term was *monitor* (from Latin *monere* 'to warn, advise'), or *prepositor*, from Latin *praepositus* 'person placed in charge', recorded as early as the sixteenth century. This is also the source of *provost*, a general term for the head of an organization, but now chiefly used of Oxbridge colleges, public schools, and cathedral chapters; in Scotland, the word is used for the head of a regional council, in a similar way to *mayor* (from Latin *major* 'greater').

A college gets its name from Latin *collegium* 'fraternity', from Latin *collega* 'partner'—literally one chosen alongside another, from *col-* 'together' and *legere* 'to choose'. The term *academy* is more common in Scotland; it is a borrowing of Akademia, a garden near Athens where Plato taught philosophy during the fourth century BC. The garden was named after an ancient Greek hero called Akademos; Plato's school took its name from that of the garden, and the word subsequently became a general term for a place of learning.

Teacher (from the verb *to teach* 'show, direct, point out'—related to *token*) has been used for an instructor since the fourteenth century. If you need to supplement your school education, you might call upon the services of a *tutor*—originally a guardian appointed to offer protection to a young person, from Latin *tueri* 'to guard'. In Anglo-Saxon schools the correct term was *lareow* 'teaching slave', from *lar* 'teaching' (ancestor of *lore*) and *þeow* 'slave'. A slightly more respectful alternative was *mægster*, the origin of *master*. The Old English word is a borrowing of Latin *magister* 'teacher' (literally 'greater person'), which is also the source of *magistrate*. Schools are overseen by the *headteacher* or *headmaster/mistress*, assisted by a *vice-master/mistress*, from Latin *vice* 'in place of'—as in *vice-president* and even *viscount* (originally *vice-count*)—or *deputy head*. Older terms for this role include the *subpreceptor* and *usher*—from Latin *ostium* 'door' (via Old French *ussier*)—this was originally the name for a servant in charge of admitting people into a room, or conducting them to their seats, as an usher still does at a wedding. Although it is now used to describe someone with an excessive concern for minor details, often stemming from a desire to showcase their own knowledge, the word *pedant* was originally a term for a teacher. Where *pedant* has taken on negative connotations of excessive fussiness, the word *meticulous*—which now denotes a concern for precision and detail in a positive sense—originally had the negative sense of 'fearful' or 'timid' (from Latin *metus* 'fear').

Pupil is from Latin *pupillus* 'orphan', from *pupus* 'boy'. The feminine equivalent was *pupa*, which could also mean 'doll'; this is the sense that lies behind the use of the word *pupil* to refer to the opening in the centre of the eye. The connection is that when you look into someone's eyes, you are greeted with a tiny reflection of yourself, thought to resemble a small doll. In Old English the word *disciple* could also be used of a student but became better known as a follower of Jesus Christ. *Disciple* is the source of *discipline*, meaning both 'field of study' and 'system of conduct'. In the Middle Ages *clerk* was commonly used (as in Chaucer's Clerk of Oxford in the *Canterbury Tales*)—from Latin *clericus*. The fondness for French words in the eighteenth century led to a brief period of use of *eleve*, from French *élève* 'pupil' (derived from *élever* 'to bring up'—related to *elevate* and *elevator*).

Someone who has left school is known as an *alumnus*; this term was first used to refer to a current student, deriving from the Latin word for a foster-son, protégé, or pupil. The word goes back to the verb *alere* 'to nourish', also the root of *aliment*, an archaic term meaning 'nourishment, food' (preserved in *alimentary canal*), and *alimony*—a maintenance payment to a divorced spouse. An *alumnus* (feminine *alumna*) may refer to a former school as an *alma mater*, literally 'nourishing mother'—a name given by the Romans to goddesses who were regarded as nurturing mother figures.

The set of subjects studied at school is known as a *syllabus*. This Latin word meant 'list'; it was originally the term used by the Greeks to refer to a label attached to a roll identifying its contents—similar in function to the title printed on the spine of a book today. From this, the word came to be used of the list of subjects studied for a particular *curriculum*—originally the word for a racing chariot or a race course, from Latin *currere* 'to run'. A number of subjects end in *-logy*; this goes back to the Greek word *logos* 'word, discourse', and *legein* 'to speak', and refers to the branch of knowledge mastered by someone who speaks of this subject. So *sociology* is the study of society (Latin *socius* 'fellow, companion'); *geology* is the study of the physical world (Greek *ge* 'earth'); *biology* is the study of living organisms (from Greek *bios* 'life').

Chemistry, the study of the substances out of which matter is composed, takes its name from the much more scientifically dubious practice of *alchemy*—the pseudo-science seeking to turn base metals into gold. A *chemist* was originally an *alchemist*; this word is ultimately from Arabic *al kimiya* 'the art of transmuting metals'; the change in form came about when it was correctly recognized that the first element, *al*, was in fact the Arabic definite article equivalent to *the*. *Physics* is from Latin *physicus* 'natural'; *physica* was the Latin term for natural science (from Greek *phusis* 'nature'), from which we get *physic*, an obsolete term for the science of medicine—think of the Doctor of Physic who is called in to observe the sleepwalking Lady Macbeth in Shakespeare's play. *Science* is from Latin *scire* 'to know', reflecting its origins as a term encompassing all kinds of learning.

Just as *physics* was formerly *physic*, so *mathematics* was originally *mathematic*; this word is from Greek *mathematikos*, which is ultimately derived from the verb *manthanein* 'to learn'. *Geometry* is from Greek *geometria* 'the science of measuring', while *arithmetic* goes back to Greek *arithmein* 'to count' (from *arithmos* 'number'); in the medieval period it was mistakenly confused with Latin *ars metrica* 'art of measure', producing the form *arsmetrike* (a gift to bawdy punsters like Chaucer); it was not until the sixteenth century that the form *arithmetic* emerged. *Algebra* originally referred to the surgical process of resetting bone fractures, originating in Arabic *al-jabr*: 'the reunion of broken pieces' or 'the restoration of anything missing'. The word *algorithm* is based upon the name of a ninth-century Arab mathematician known as al-Kwarizmi, meaning 'the native of Khorezm'—now Khiva in Uzbekistan. Initially used to refer to the decimal system of numbers, the form *algorithm* is probably due to influence from the Greek word *arithmos*. Modern English *digit*, signifying a number between 0 and 9, is from the Latin word *digitus* meaning 'finger'. The connection between these two is the universal practice of counting using our fingers. Another early form of counting relied on the use of an *abacus*; this was originally a board covered with sand on which calculations or diagrams could be drawn, and sums could be reckoned using pebbles. From this we get the word *calculus*, the name of a branch of mathematics, which originates in the diminutive form of Latin *calx* 'pebble', referring to the small stones used for counting on an abacus. While the numbers themselves are of Old English origin, *zero* goes back to the Arabic word *ṣifr*, meaning 'empty', which is also the source of *cipher*—used initially of the symbol for zero, then of someone of no importance, and now most commonly of writing in code.

If all this science and maths is making your brain ache, perhaps it's time for a physical work-out. *PE*, or *physical education*, usually takes place in a *gymnasium*; this gets its name from Greek *gumnazein* 'exercise naked' (Greek *gumnos* 'naked'), because of the practice of Greek athletes competing in the *nude* (from Latin *nudus* 'naked'). Or perhaps you could get some exercise by running down the corridor. If you find a teacher attempting to stop you, you should point out that running in corridors is perfectly acceptable, since *corridor* is from Italian *corridore* 'running place' (Latin *currere* 'to run').

But it's in the school playground that we find the richest linguistic treasures—in the constantly evolving slang terms, as well as the traditional rhymes that are passed on from generation to generation.

The Playground

A dispute concerning ownership rights might invoke the principle that a lost item becomes the property of the first person to find it, as enshrined in the rhyme *Finders keepers, losers weepers*, which comes in a variety of regional guises, such as *Findie, findie, keeps it; losie, losie, seeks it*, or *Finders keeps; losers greets* (a Scots word meaning 'cry'). Other versions codify the taboo against attempting to take back objects claimed in this manner, such as *Findings keepings; taking back's stealings*.

Another method of claiming ownership or precedence involves being the first to exclaim *Bags I*, or *Bagsy*. Once again, a number of regional alternatives are attested, including *ballow, barley, bollars, chaps, fogs, jigs it*, and *nab it*. The best-known contemporary equivalent is probably *shotgun*, which originated in a claim to ride in the front passenger seat—known as the *shotgun seat* because it is the position typically occupied by an armed guard. If ownership of an item is being voluntarily renounced—presumably because it no longer works or tastes disgusting—children may employ the Latin *quis* 'who', to which the first person to respond *ego* (Latin for 'I') is entitled to lay claim. If that may seem to imply impressive levels of Latinity among schoolchildren, this appearance is some-what undermined by the existence of the equivalent phrase *I egoed it*. A less decorous method of redistribution sees the donor launching the object into the air and shouting *scrambles!*, and then retreating to admire the resulting melee.

Of all the many playground games, one of the simplest and most durable involves a single child chasing a pack; when the pursuer catches one of the children, he or she becomes the pursuer. This game has been known by a variety of names, including *tig, tag, touch, it, he, kingy*; in Cornwall it is called *widdy, widdy way*—from the following rhyme with which the game begins: 'Widdy, widdy, way, Is a very pretty play, Once, twice, three times, And all run away.' Playground rhymes and songs may also be incorporated into games. In the game known as *Hi cockalorum*, the exclamation *hey cocka-lorum, jig, jig, jig!* is shouted by a player when leapfrogging over the backs of the others; this originated in the refrain of a popular song from the early nineteenth century. An important item in a child's vocabulary for this and many other playground games is the truce term that is shouted when a child wants to pause the game—to tie up a shoe-lace, catch breath, or to investigate a grazed knee—regional variants include *fains, scribs, cree, barley, kings, crosses, skinch*, and *keys*. Alongside these simple games are rather more sinister pastimes that would cause a school inspector to blanch, such as the thankfully obsolete *knifey*, in which children throw knives into the ground so as to just miss their opponent's feet.

Another linguistically rich category comprises the names given to various pranks. Particularly long-lasting is the game in which a child raps loudly on the front door of a house and then runs away, leaving a confused householder gazing down an empty street—the aim of the game being to escape without being spotted. More than sixty names have been recorded for this dubious practice; these range from the straightforwardly descriptive *ring-bell-scoot, tap-door-run, bing bang skoosh*, to the more unusual *cheeky nellie, jinksy tat, rosy apple, black and white rabbit*, and *squashed tomato* (also recorded as a name for the game better known today as *sardines*). In London and the south-east the dominant name is *knock down ginger*—perhaps based on the common use of *ginger* as a nick-name for someone with ginger hair. Pranks like these require the appointment of a lookout—termed a *weany, spy-eye, crow-boy, rookie*, or *dodger*, whose job it was to keep *cave* (Latin 'beware') or *nix, dousy, Kate*, or *conk*.

But while these games and their associated calls have stood the test of time, other children's slang dates very quickly. Words that were once the height of cool, like *ace, beezer, bonza, whizzing, rotten, swiz*, and *chiz*, survive today only in the stories of Geoffrey Willans's fictional schoolboy Nigel Molesworth, the curse of St Custard's. School slang also has a strongly regional element; a young lout or *yob* (formed in Cockney back-slang from *boy*) may be known as a *pikey* in London, a *scally* in the north-west, a *charva* in the north-east, and a *ned* in the west of Scotland. But some regional words have spread more widely; the equivalent term *chav*, which originated in the south-east in the 1990s, is now used widely through the UK. Although it is often claimed to be a short-ened form of Chatham, a town in Kent where it may have originated, it is probably based upon the Romany *chavo* 'boy, youth'. Also of Romany origin is *cushty*, a general purpose term meaning 'good, fine, brilliant', best known today from its use by Del Boy of the TV sitcom *Only Fools and Horses*. Originating in Romany *kushto*, the form it has taken in English may be due to influence from the similar word *cushy*—borrowed from Urdu *k̲u̲šī* 'pleasure, convenience'—which entered English in the nineteenth century. Another term favoured by Del Boy is *pukka*, meaning 'genuine' or 'excellent', a borrowing of the Hindi word *pakkā* 'cooked, ripe'. This word was subsequently taken up by TV chef Jamie Oliver in the catchphrase *pukka tukka*; given the word's etymological origins, this phrase was more appropriate than he realized. Talk of pukka tukka takes us to the serious business of eating and drinking, to be covered in the following section.

PART III

Eating & Drinking

CHAPTER 11

Breaktimes

The mid-morning break or *elevenses* is traditionally a time for what Pooh Bear would call a little smackerel of something. Despite being warned of the dangers of snacking between meals, we've been enjoying our *nuncheons, mixtums, refections, bevers, waterings,* and *lite bites* for centuries. Another of Pooh Bear's favourite expressions (along with 'What about lunch?' and 'Help yourself, Pooh') is *a little something*—first recorded in the sixteenth century. The *second breakfast* beloved of J. R. R. Tolkien's hobbits—Bilbo Baggins is sitting down to a nice little second breakfast when Gandalf walks in and disrupts his peaceful existence—is first recorded in the eighteenth century. Since you've been hard at work for at least a couple of hours by now, you may also be in need of some artificial stimulation in the form of caffeine.

Coffee

The word *coffee* is from Arabic *qahwa*, originally referring to a type of wine. It entered Europe via Turkish *kahveh* in the early seventeenth century, appearing earliest in the Italian *caffè*; the English *coffee*, with an 'o' rather than an 'a', was probably derived from the Dutch adoption of the word, *koffie*. Over the last four centuries, the stimulating beverage has been available from *coffee houses, shops,* and *bars*—ranging from the upmarket *coffee palaces* and *parlours* to the more functional *coffee stalls, stands*, and even *barrows*. The drink has had its detractors, as is implied by some of the less flattering nicknames: *syrup of soot, ninny-broth, Turkey gruel*, and *mud*.

Since the eighteenth century *coffee* has also been used to refer to a light meal including the drink—known in early twentieth-century USA as *coffee and*—or the taking of coffee at the end of a meal. A *coffee-klatsch*, based on the German *Kaffeeklatsch* 'coffee gossip', is a US term for a coffee party. The *coffee jacket*, worn by women when drinking coffee, is first recorded in 1901—a reference in the *Daily Chronicle* suggesting that the drink was surpassing tea in popularity: 'The newest tea jackets have changed their names to coffee jackets.' *Coffee cups* are first recorded in the eighteenth century—these were originally larger than the coffee cups used today, though probably not as substantial as the *coffee dish*— plated with silver—recorded in a seventeenth-century edition of the *London Gazette*. The *coffee set*, chinaware used specifically for serving coffee, has been available since the late eighteenth century.

Various developments have changed the way that the coffee is produced. Slow-brewed coffee is made using a *filter, cafetière*, or *percolator* (from Latin *percolare* 'to filter, strain'—the stem verb *colare* also survives in the metal strainer known as a *colander*). *Espresso* derives from the Italian *caffè espresso* 'pressed-out coffee'. This word is often mistakenly assimilated to the more common English word *express*, resulting in *expresso*. This spelling is now sufficiently common to have been accepted as a variant in a number of dictionaries—much to the chagrin of their readers, who have made their feelings clear in hostile posts on their bulletin boards. *Cappuccino*, made using frothed milk with added chocolate sprinkles, is so called because the colour of the drink resembles that of the habits worn by Capuchin friars—an offshoot of the Franciscan brotherhood named for their distinctive pointed hoods (Italian *capuccio*). Also of Italian origin is the *caffè latte*, now more commonly abbreviated to *latte*, made with steamed milk rather than water, from the Italian word meaning 'milk'. Italian *latte* originates in Latin *lac*, the source of English *lactose* and *lactic*—as in *lactic acid*. *Latte macchiato*, an espresso with a small serving of frothy milk, gets its name from the Italian *macchiato* 'stained', describing the way the milk appears to be stained by the addition of the coffee. Italian does not have a complete monopoly on coffee terms, however; the *cortado*, an espresso with a dash of steamed milk, is Spanish in origin, deriving from *cortar* 'to cut'. German is the source of the wonderfully named *Schlagobers*, a term for coffee with whipped cream, from *schlagen* 'to beat' and the Austrian dialect word *obers* 'cream'. French has given coffee drinkers the *frappé*, from a French word meaning 'iced', for those rare occasions when the weather is sufficiently warm. The blend *frappuccino* is an invention of the coffee industry; it was coined by US coffee giant Starbucks. The Seattle-based firm has prior experience of linguistic inventiveness—the corporation is named after the first mate in Herman Melville's novel *Moby-Dick* (1851), after the name of the whaling ship, the *Pequod*, was rejected on the grounds that people might object to drinking something that sounds like 'pee-quod'.

No coffee break is complete without something to snack upon. Perhaps it's time for a visit to the local *pâtisserie*, the French word for a shop selling freshly made pastries, from Latin *pasticium* 'pasty'. Here you could indulge in such delicacies as an *eclair*; this name comes from a French word meaning 'bolt of lightning', and may refer to the fact that eclairs don't last long—a feature famously captured by the Chambers Dictionary in its definition: 'long in shape but short in duration'. The layered puff pastry slice filled with cream known as *millefeuille* is an abbreviation of the earlier *gâteau de mille-feuilles* 'cake of a thousand leaves'—a reference to its multiple folds and layers. The *crêpe* is from the French term for a pancake, derived from Latin *crispus* 'curled'. The *macaroon*, French *macaron*, takes its name from the same Italian word that gives us *macaroni*. The invention of the rich sponge cake known as the *madeleine* has been attributed to a nineteenth-century French pastry chef called Madeleine Paumier. The word is now also used to refer to something strongly nostalgic, with reference to a famous passage in Marcel Proust's novel *Swann's Way* (1908): 'And suddenly the memory returns. The taste was that of the little crumb of madeleine...my aunt Léonie used to give me, dipping it first in her own cup of real or of lime-flower tea.'

Perhaps the nearest patisserie is too far, or perhaps the only thing that will satisfy your 11 a.m. craving is a slab of chocolate. When we think of chocolate today, we picture the hard confectionery that comes in bars, either on its own or as a covering for other types of sweet substances. But chocolate was first introduced into Britain in the early seventeenth century in the form of a hot drink, in which the chocolate was mixed with water or milk. In 1664 Samuel Pepys made the following entry in his diary: 'To a Coffee-house to drink Jocolatte, very good.' The word entered English from Spanish, but it ultimately derives from *chocolatl*, a word used in the Nahuatl language to refer to food made using cacao seeds. Pepys's spelling of the word may appear odd to us today, but spellings with an initial 'j' are recorded into the nineteenth century in English dialects. While Pepys may have been forced to purchase his first cup of hot chocolate from a coffee house, it wouldn't be long before he and his fellow Londoners could frequent one of the numerous *chocolate houses* that became such a feature of fashionable life in the eighteenth century. This period witnessed the emergence of the *chocolate cup*, specifically intended for drinking chocolate, the *chocolate mill*, a hand utensil for stirring the drink, and the *chocolate pot*, in which the drink was made or served. A *chocolate teapot*, however, is something quite different; rather than describing a vessel in which hot chocolate was made, it alludes to any completely impractical invention, since the teapot would melt once the boiling water was added.

Alternatively, you might prefer to have a *biscuit*—from Latin *bis* 'twice' and *coctus* 'cooked', so called because they were first baked and then dried out in an oven. Many of the best-known biscuit varieties are named after their ingredients, such as the *ginger snap*, but others have more interesting origins. *Hobnob* originated as a variant form of *hab or nab*, a contraction of *habben or nabben* 'to have or to have not'— first recorded as used by Shakespeare to mean 'give or take'. The phrase later became a toast used by people to drink to each other's health, from which the modern sense of mixing socially (especially with people belonging to a higher social group) evolved.

For a slightly more substantial snack you could treat yourself to a piece of cake. The British obsession with cake has left its impression on the English language in numerous ways. The belief that the mouth was designed principally for its consumption is suggested by the slang term *cake-hole*. Something that is easily achieved is *a piece of cake*, the good life is known as *cakes and ale* (an allusion to Sir Toby Belch's scornful riposte to the puritanical Malvolio in Shakespeare's *Twelfth Night*: 'Dost thou thinke, because thou art virtuous, there shall be no more cakes and ale?'), *the icing on the cake* refers to an unnecessary but desirable enhancement (perhaps with *a cherry on the top*), and to win is *to take the cake*, although this is now more commonly used ironically, while *biscuit* has come to replace *cake*.

If you are put off choosing the cake option because of the well-known proverb *You can't have your cake and eat it*, do not be deterred. Many people are confused by this expression, since, having acquired a cake, expecting to eat it seems an entirely reasonable proposition. The reason for the confusion is that the original form of the phrase has been reversed in its modern incarnation; in a sixteenth-century book of proverbs it appears as follows: 'Wolde ye bothe eate your cake, and haue your cake?' The idea, then, is that once you have eaten your cake, you can no longer continue to possess it; that is, sometimes you are forced to choose between two irreconcilable options. Similar idioms can be traced in other national cultures, albeit with their own regional twist. In French the equivalent is *vouloir le beurre et l'argent du beurre*, 'to want the butter and the money from (selling) the butter', to which the extension *et le sourire de la crémière* 'and a smile from the shopkeeper' can be appended for added effect. In Romania it is impossible to *reconcile both the cabbage and the goat*, while in Italy one cannot have *the barrel full and the wife drunk*. In Germany you can't dance at two weddings at the same time, while the Czech version refers to the impossibility of simultaneously occupying two stools. Given the ubiquity of the phrase, it seems significant that it is only in the English version that the object of desire is a cake.

The British love affair with cake extends to the monarchy. The humble *Victoria sponge*, or *sandwich*, was named for Queen Victoria, who was keen on a slice with her afternoon cuppa. The *Battenberg* cake was invented to celebrate the marriage of Louis of Battenberg into the British Royal family in the 1880s; Prince Louis changed his name to the anglicized Mountbatten during the First World War, in response to anti-German sentiment, but the cake has retained its German associations. The *marzipan* with which it is coated is from Italian *marzapane*, which originates in the name of a port in what is now Myanmar. The port of Martaban exported sweets in specially made jars, which came to be known by the Italian form *marzapanes*. A later development saw the name for the jar transferred to its contents. When it was first introduced into English it was known by the anglicized form *marchpane* (a word revived by Philip Pullman in the *His Dark Materials* trilogy); in the nineteenth century it was reintroduced in the Italian form, giving us *marzipan*.

Should you decide to choose a *scone*, be warned—nothing divides English speakers so much as the question of how to pronounce this word. Originally a large round cake eaten in Scotland, its name derives from the Middle Dutch *schoonbrot* 'fine bread'. Today scones are enjoyed around the world, but there are clear regional divisions as to how the word should be pronounced. In the US the word is more usually sounded to rhyme with *phone*, whereas in South Africa, Australia, and New Zealand it more commonly rhymes with *gone*.

In Britain both pronunciations are widely used, though the one rhyming with *gone* is more usually heard in the north of England, while that rhyming with *phone* is more commonly used in the south. But this simple account of the regional distribution belies the level of passion with which speakers consider their own pronunciation to be correct and the alternative to be wrong. Hearing someone use the alternative is enough to make a sane person completely lose their cool, or, to use a happily appropriate phrase, *go off their scone*.

The mid-morning break is also a chance for smokers to huddle together in the cold in some fittingly *unsalubrious* (from Latin *salus* 'health') spot and get a nicotine fix. *Nicotine*, the name given to the active ingredient in the tobacco leaf, is named after Jean Nicot (1530–1600), the French ambassador to Lisbon and compiler of one of the first dictionaries of French, who introduced tobacco into France in the 1560s.

Smoking

Cigar, first attested in the early eighteenth century in the form *seegar*, is from Spanish *cigarro*, possibly related to *cigarra* 'cicada', perhaps on account of similarities in shape between a roll of tobacco leaf and the insect, or from the Mayan word *sik'ar* 'smoking'. *Cigarette* did not appear until a century later; the word is borrowed direct from the French diminutive of *cigar*, and so means 'little cigar'. The slang term *fag* is a contraction of *fag-end*, earlier referring to the last remaining part of anything that has been all but used up, but now specifically to the butt of a cigarette. The *pipe* gets its name from the word used for any tubular object intended to convey fluids or gases; the word is from Old English *pipe* 'musical tube', ultimately from Latin *pipare* 'to chirp'. Pipe-smoking has given the English language several useful phrases: *to put someone's pipe out*, meaning 'foil or frustrate', and that most crushing of put-downs: *put that in your pipe and smoke it*—meaning 'put up with it, like it or not'.

Also of Spanish origin is the word *tobacco* (Spanish *tabaco*), although the origins of the word remain disputed. One theory derives it from a Carib term for a pipe in which tobacco was smoked, another that it originated in a Taino word for a basic form of cigar. As well as being smoked the tobacco leaves may be chewed, or snorted in the powdered form known as *snuff*—a contraction of the Dutch *snuftabak*. Although the practice of snuff-taking has largely fallen out of fashion, its earlier centrality to fashionable dining is apparent from the many accoutrements recorded in the eighteenth and nineteenth centuries—*snuff box, snuff shop, snuff spoon*, as well as the term *snuff hand*—referring to the hand with which one takes snuff. Although phrases like *beat to snuff*, meaning 'batter completely', and *in high snuff*, 'in high spirits', have fallen out of use, modern English still employs the phrase *up to snuff* to describe something that is considered to be 'up to the required standard'.

Today we are just as likely to catch smokers *drawing, pulling*, or *puffing* on something that looks more like a piccolo than a cigarette. The practice of *vaping*—the term for inhaling the vapour produced by an e-cigarette—became so popular in 2014 that Oxford Dictionaries labelled *vape* their word of the year. In April 2014 the UK's first vape café—The Vape Lab—was opened in London; the emergence of new compounds such as *vape lounge* and *vape shop* further testified to the establishment of vaping. In order to distinguish it from the older technology, the retronym (a new coinage intended to distinguish an existing word from a more recent one) *tobacco cigarette* was introduced. But while vaping might have seemed like a trendy and cool pursuit back in 2014, its fortunes seem less assured today. The Vape Lab has long since closed; for all its hype, perhaps *vape* was just too close to *vapid* (from Latin *vapidus* 'having lost its freshness, flat') to last.

Now that you are experiencing your caffeine, sugar, or nicotine rush—or a combination of all three—it is time to turn to your co-workers and engage in small talk. The safest place to begin is with the favourite topic of all British conversations: the weather.

Discussing the Weather

It is often remarked that the British are obsessed with the weather and that all interactions will inevitably involve some reference to the current conditions—usually in negative and gloomy terms. Indeed, the importance the British place on the weather is apparent from the many idioms and expressions that make reference to it. When we are sick we are *under the weather*; when we recover we are *right as rain*. During a rare moment of *optimism* (Latin *optimus* 'best'), we greet an unexpected upside of a negative situation with the phrase *Every cloud has a silver lining*; a more lugubrious outlook might prompt us to lament: *It never rains but it pours*. A true friend is one who stands by us *come rain or shine*, while a *fair-weather friend* is nowhere to be found during the tough times.

Along with the rain, clouds form a pretty constant feature of the English weather. This word derives from Old English *clud*, although this was originally the term for a rock or hill. The Anglo-Saxons drew upon the Old Norse word *sky* to refer to a cloud; but when this word shifted to its modern meaning, the word *cloud* came to take its place. The shift in meaning of Old Norse *sky* had a further impact on two Old English words that had hitherto been used to refer to the sky. The result was that Old English *heofon* came to refer to the Christian heavens, and *wolcen* fell out of use entirely. Cloud forma-tions are officially classified into the following major categories according to their appearance: *cirrus*, a wispy or tufted cloud (from Latin *cirrus* 'curl'), *cumulus*, heaped up or puffy clouds (from Latin *cumulus* 'heap'), *stratus*, flat and smooth (from Latin *stratus* 'strewn'), and *nimbus*, a rain cloud (from Latin *nimbus* 'cloud').

There is a linguistic urban legend that claims that Eskimos have hundreds of words for snow. They don't, and even if they did it wouldn't be a very surprising fact. After all, English is pretty well endowed with terms to describe rain—*shower, drizzle, downpour, torrent, pouring, flood*—and that's not counting dialect words like *mizzle, smur,* and *dag.* Winds may be described as a gentle *breeze* (from Old Spanish *briza* 'north-westerly wind') or a stronger *gale*, originally a *gale-wind*, perhaps from an Old Norse word meaning 'frantic'. Stronger winds may be termed *hurricanes, typhoons, cyclones,* or *tornadoes.* A *hurricane*, the term for a tropical storm in the Caribbean, is from Spanish *huracán*, probably originating in the Taino word *hurakán* 'god of the storm'. The *typhoon*, the term for a tropical storm in the Indian or western Pacific oceans, gets its name from an Arabic word meaning 'whirlwind', a meaning that was supported by the Chinese dialect *tai fung* 'big wind'. *Tornado*, denoting a tropical storm recorded in the Atlantic Ocean, is from Spanish *tronada* 'thunderstorm'. The *cyclone*, a wind rotating inwards, is from the Greek word *kuklos* 'circle', the same word that gives us *cycle.* The phrase *halcyon days*, which refers nostalgically to an idyllic time in the past, was originally a reference to a time of calm. The word *halcyon* is from Greek *alkuon* 'kingfisher', a bird that was thought to be able to calm the winds and waves during its breeding period.

The coffee break is also a time to exchange gossip; this word originates in the Old English *godsibb* 'godparent'—the second element, meaning 'related by blood', is still found today in *sibling.* The tendency for discussion of the latest celebrity break-up, political scandal, or sporting event to take place at the office water-cooler has given rise to terms like *water-cooler story, water-cooler TV,* and *water-cooler moment.*

A parallel development can be traced in the way *scuttlebutt*, the nautical term for the cask of drinking-water kept on a ship, came to refer to idle gossip and *rumour* (from Latin *rumor* 'noise').

Perhaps you've had quite enough chatting with real people and instead prefer to turn to your virtual friends and followers on social media. Technically, the difference between friends and followers concerns reciprocity—a follower can follow you without you needing to reciprocate (although under the terms of a *F4F*, or *follow for follow*, this would be expected), whereas a Facebook friend can only become your friend with your consent. Not all followers are friendly, however; lurking in cyberspace are numerous *trolls, sockpuppets*, and *sealions*—accounts designed to post and promote deliberately provocative and offensive material and viewpoints, and to derail genuine attempts at debate.

Social Media

The *meme*, an image with a comic caption that is spread widely over the internet, takes its name from a term coined by the geneticist Richard Dawkins. For Dawkins *meme* referred to aspects of behaviour or culture that were passed between individuals within a society by non-genetic means, such as imitation. The word originates in the ancient Greek word *mimema*, meaning 'that which is imitated'—also the source of *mimesis*, a technical term describing the artistic and literary representation of the world, and *mime*, 'imitate, copy'. Having chosen to derive his new coinage from the Greek root *mimeme*, Dawkins decided to abbreviate it to *meme* in order to enable a clearer parallel with *gene*—apologizing to his classicist friends in the process.

The *hashtag*, or the *hash* or *hash mark*, probably originates in the verb *hatch*—to shade an area with parallel lines, perhaps with some influence from the similar *hash* 'cut into small pieces'. The symbol is sometimes referred to as the *octothorp*, a term that was coined within the Bell Laboratories telecom company—the *octo* element may have been chosen to reflect the symbol's eight points (Latin *octo* 'eight'). Also coined by a software engineer is *Bluetooth*: the name given to the wireless communication technology. The term originates in the epithet given to King Harald I of Denmark (*c*.910–985), who united a collection of Scandinavian territories under Danish rule. This process of unification was thought to be similar to the way in which Bluetooth technology enables communication between different electronic devices. The Bluetooth symbol also draws upon this ancient Scandinavian connection, since it comprises the two runic symbols that make up King Harald's initials.

The word *selfie* can be traced back to its apparent first use in 2002, when an Australian man posted an image of his injured face, after falling down some steps having drunk heavily at a friend's 21st birthday party. In the post he apologized for the poor quality of the picture, which should not be attributed to drunkenness, but rather to its being a selfie. Although we cannot be certain that this was the word's first use, the Australian love of the 'ie' shortening—attested in words like *barbie* 'barbecue', *postie* 'postman', and *tinnie* 'tin of beer'—make this a likely provenance. But while the word may have been coined to describe a photograph taken by someone who features in it, this meaning has shifted in recent years to encompass other kinds of photographs taken with a smartphone and posted on social media.

Social media posts that generate considerable interest by being shared, liked, and retweeted are said to be *trending* or to have *gone viral*—likening the speed with which they are transmitted to that of an infectious virus (from Latin *virus* 'poisonous liquid', used to refer to a snake's venom). It is this potential that lies behind the success of *milkshake duck*—the term for someone who is catapulted to fame but then quickly discovered to have a shady past. It was coined by an Australian comedian in a tweet about a cute duck that drinks milkshake but is shortly afterwards uncovered as a racist. But while the term was runner-up in Oxford Dictionaries Word of the Year for 2017, it remains to be seen how long it will remain in use.

The potential of social media for spreading neologisms that capture a new concept for which there is no equivalent term was harnessed by a group of lexicographers and PR executives who set out to coin a word that would go on to be adopted throughout the English-speaking world. The word they came up with was *phubbing*—a blend of *phone* and *snubbing*—to describe that well-known image of a couple seated together in a romantic restaurant deep in conversation on their mobile phones. But, despite capturing a recognized concept, the success of their coinage may be undermined by its lack of *euphony* (from Greek *euphonia* 'well-sounding').

Checking email inevitably means spending a considerable amount of time deleting messages congratulating you on winning the lottery, or offering you lucrative business deals in exchange for your bank details. The term *spam* is derived from the name of a tinned luncheon meat, whose name is a blend of *spiced ham*; its association with flooding individuals with unwanted messages comes from a Monty Python sketch set in a café in which Spam forms the principal ingredient of every dish on the menu and so cannot be avoided. 'Have you got anything without Spam in it?' asks a customer who doesn't like Spam—'Spam, Egg, Sausage, and Spam hasn't got much Spam in it,' replies the waitress.

If communicating with your Facebook friends and Twitter followers using English is just too much hassle, you can always fall back on the universal language of the smiling face—otherwise known as *emoji*. Indeed, it's possible that the increasing development and adoption of emoji pictograms, which allow speakers to communicate without the need for language, means that in the future we will have no need for the English language at all.☺ I've used the winky-face emoji here to indicate that I'm joking. But am I? After all, while there are over a billion users of English in the world today, this number is positively dwarfed by the number of smartphone users, ninety per cent of whom make regular use of emoji.

Emoji

While recent years have seen the proliferation of emoji, they are not a new phenomenon. They were originally developed in Japan in the 1990s for use by teenagers on their pagers; the word *emoji* derives from the Japanese *e* 'picture' and *moji* 'character, letter'. Its successful integration into English has no doubt been facilitated by its resemblance to other words that begin with the *e*-prefix—a contraction of *electronic*—found in words like *email, e-cigarette*, and *e-commerce*. Their success is a direct consequence of the digital medium in which they are used. Electronic communication is a form of writing that resembles a casual conversation more than formal prose, often taking place in real time with a known recipient, but lacking the extra-linguistic cues such as facial expression, tone of voice, hand gestures, that help to convey meaning in face-to-face interactions. New methods of encoding such features of communication emerged to enable senders to include non-linguistic interjections—*sigh*—and physical responses: *facepalm*. Raising one's voice is made possible by the use of capital letters, while additional spaces add a dash of condescension: D O Y O U U N D E R S T A N D ?

The *emoticon* (a blend of *emotion* and *icon*), or *smiley*, grew out of a need to transmit a broader range of attitudes. It first appeared on computer science bulletin boards in the early 1980s, where the combination of keyboard strokes :-) were used to mark jokes, while :-(indicated seriousness. Despite being dismissed by punctuation crusader Lynne Truss as a 'paltry substitute for expressing oneself properly', emoticons developed to convey a wider range of emotions, including a straight face : | and ones expressing surprise >: o and scepticism >: \.

Emoji have come to replace the comparative crudity of the emoticon, enabling the representation of a far greater range of expressions with less ambiguity. Where the double smiley :-))— used to express increased hilarity—runs the risk of appearing to imply your recipient has a double chin, emoji offer a variety of grinning faces, including ones crying with laughter, or with smiling eyes. While a similar attitude may be rendered by the ubiquitous *LOL* ('laughing out loud'), this has the disadvantage of being potentially misconstrued as 'lots of love', with embarrassing results. Acronyms describing increased levels of amusement, such as *ROFL* or *ROTFL* ('rolling on the floor laughing'), are less well known and considerably less snappy.

The most commonly employed emoji are the smiling, frowning, and winking faces—used to show when a writer is happy, sad, or joking. The desire to flag when a message is intended to be ironic or sarcastic is not new; in 1887 Ambrose Bierce, author of *The Devil's Dictionary*, proposed the introduction of the *snigger point* (or *mark of cachinnation* 'laughing loudly')—a horizontal round bracket resembling a smile—which would be appended to all 'jocular' or 'ironical' sentences.

But where the use of emoji has grown out of a radical move to shake off the constraints of written language, users remain restricted by the numbers and types of emoji available. The release of new emoji is subject to the approval of the Unicode Consortium, a kind of Académie Française for emoji. Such deci-sions are frequently contentious, given the lack of representation of certain ethnic groups, their cultures, and their religions; it is only recently that it has become possible to choose from a range of skin tones.

While recent updates have enabled greater cultural diversity, the representation of foods, clothes, and places of worship remain highly westernized. However representative emoji become, it is not possible to legislate for the cultural sensitivity of their users. The pine decoration emoji, representing *kadomatsu*—placed at the front of Japanese homes at New Year to welcome spirits in the hope of a plentiful harvest—is regularly used in the West as an offensive gesture, since it resembles a raised middle finger.

But for emoji to become a fully-fledged language in its own right we would need a vastly greater number of characters. At present the system remains too crude to represent all but the most straightforward concepts, as is apparent from the rendering of Herman Melville's classic novel *Moby-Dick* in emoji. In *Emoji Dick*, the novel's famous opening sentence, 'Call me Ishmael', is rendered somewhat cryptically by a series of icons showing a telephone, a man with a moustache, a boat, a whale, and an OK sign. Something has surely been lost in translation.

♥

CHAPTER 12

Mealtimes

Just as English speakers are divided by their pronunciation of *scone*, so too are they by the terms used to refer to the daily meals. The midday meal is known to many as *lunch*—this word originally referred to a thick piece or hunk (of bread or meat) and is probably a borrowing of the Spanish word *lonja*, meaning 'slice'. The longer form, *luncheon*, is recorded earlier with reference to the midday meal; the shorter form of *lunch* was first introduced in the 1820s. But while *luncheon* now sounds very posh, if not slightly affected, back in the 1820s it was the other way around—*luncheon* was the usual term, while *lunch* was considered a fashionable affectation. Dr Johnson suggested that the word originated in *clutch* or *clunch*, and referred to 'as much food as one's hand can hold'—not the most hygienic way of serving food. Others refer to the midday meal as *dinner*, from French *dîner* 'to dine'. This word is ultimately from the same root as *déjeuner* 'lunch'—its different form is a reflection of its greater age. But, while *dinner* may be used to refer to the main meal of the day— whether eaten at midday or in the evening—its use is socially loaded. Although first drafted in 1896, the relevant *OED* entry captures this shift in usage: 'The chief meal of the day, eaten originally, and still by the majority of people, about the middle of the day, but now, by the professional and fashionable classes, usually in the evening.' Even though it may sound like a very fancy affair, you should turn down an invitation to *dine with Duke Humphrey*, since this is a sixteenth-century phrase meaning 'go without dinner'.

A widespread term for the last meal of the day is *supper*; the distinction between *supper* and *dinner* being one of size and formality— *supper* generally referring to a lighter and more casual affair. But the uses of these terms can vary considerably according to region and dialect—if you are invited to supper in Scotland make sure you have eaten beforehand, since to the Scots *supper* is a light meal before bed. Although it is a borrowing from a French word, *supper* is Germanic in origin—it is from the same root as *sop*, originally a piece of bread dipped in wine or soup, and now a bribe or peace offering. This contemporary usage derives from Virgil's *Æneid*, where Æneas is able to pass Cerberus, the three-headed dog that guards the entrance to the Underworld, by feeding him a sop laced with honey and sleep-inducing herbs.

The feature of dining that is most likely to give away your social origins is that innocent square of fabric or paper that you place on your lap in case of spillages. For the aspiring member of the upper class, the correct term is *napkin* (from Old French *nape* 'tablecloth'); the alternative term, *serviette*, is considered by many to be a middle-class pretension. This social distinction is a direct result of Nancy Mitford's popularization of the concept of U and non-U; despite having been used in English since the fifteenth century, after 1950 *serviette* came to be seen as the linguistic equivalent of other middle-class affectations, such as fish knives, tea cosies, and napkin rings—serviette rings presumably being the ultimate social gaffe. If you want to sidestep this complex social minefield, the safest term to employ is *meal* (originally the name for the edible part of the grain), since this can be used at any time of the day and has few social connotations.

The standard working lunch is a *sandwich*, eaten while hunched over a desk or during a meeting. It was allegedly during a lengthy gambling session, during which he was unwilling to leave the table to eat, that John Montagu, 4th Earl of Sandwich (1718–1792), requested some cold beef between two slices of bread, with the result that his name has become synonymous with this ubiquitous bread snack. Whether the story is true or not, there's no doubting that

Montagu was on to something with this serendipitous gastronomic invention; whether he would be pleased to be remembered for his relentless gambling is less certain. The American *beefburger* was originally a *Hamburger*—the name deriving from the German city of Hamburg—but, since this connection was forgotten, the term *beef-burger* has become equally popular. A colleague that you share a sandwich with is technically your *companion*, since the word derives from Latin *com* 'together with' and *panis* 'bread'. The word *mate* is of a similar origin, since it shares a root with the word *meat* (which initially referred to all kinds of food), and was originally someone you split your food with.

Instead of a quick sandwich at your desk, you may prefer to go to a restaurant for something more substantial—if you are in a celebratory mood you might indulge in a *feast* (from Latin *festus* 'joyous'). Be wary if your festive mood should prompt you to choose a *banquet*—while this may refer to a substantial meal comprising numerous courses, its origins are considerably more abstemious. The word is originally a French term meaning 'little bench' (as it still does in *banquette*), and was initially employed to describe a light snack enjoyed between meals.

Much of the vocabulary surrounding fine dining is French in origin—its continental origins still signalled by the pronunciation. *Haute cuisine*, literally 'high cookery', refers to food produced to a very high standard; the word *cuisine* is from the French word for a kitchen. *Cordon bleu*, 'blue ribbon', was originally a ribbon worn by the knights belonging to the order of the Holy Ghost, the highest order of chivalry. In England, a *blue ribbon* (or *riband*) made of silk was worn by members of the Order of the Garter. From these uses the terms *blue ribbon* or *cordon bleu* were subsequently applied to any first-rate practitioner who has achieved distinction in a particular field. The technical term for the art of fine eating is *gastronomy*, a French borrowing that draws upon the Greek word *gaster* 'stomach', and which has been given its own English twist in the 1990s formation *gastropub*. The Greek *gaster* also appears in *gastropod* 'stomach foot', the collective term for molluscs such as snails and slugs that have a broad 'foot' running along the underside of their stomach that propels them forward. For those of you who are Francophile foodies all this talk of snails—known on menus by the French name *escargot*—will be *whetting* your appetite (which is from Old English *hwettan* 'to sharpen'). For others, this talk of edible molluscs will be having the opposite effect—perhaps even inducing another *gastro* term, *gastroenteritis*, an inflammation of the stomach.

The word *restaurant* is also of French extraction, originating in the verb *restaurer* 'to restore, bring back to health'. On being seated in the restaurant, diners are presented with a *menu*—from a French word meaning 'detailed list' (Latin *minutus* 'small'). You might choose to order from the *à la carte*, 'according to the menu', or the *prix fixe*, 'fixed price', options. In addition to your main course, you could select an *hors d'oeuvre*, a French term for an appetizer. Introduced into English in the eighteenth century, this term, meaning 'outside the work', was originally used to refer to something out of the ordinary, or additional. Its culinary use derives from the idea of a dish that is served as a supplement to the standard courses. From Italian cuisine English has adopted the term *antipasti* (the plural of *antipasto*), meaning 'before the food', from Latin *pastus* 'food'. If you are not especially hungry, you may prefer a selection of *canapés*— bite-sized pieces of bread or pastry with savoury toppings. *Canapé* is the French word for a sofa; the idea behind its use here is that the toppings were thought to resemble people sitting on a sofa.

The tendency for French culinary terms to occupy a higher regis- ter than the equivalent English ones is perhaps clearest in the French origins of *beef, pork, veal, venison,* and *mutton,* that were taken from the speech of the French noblemen who settled in Britain following the Norman Conquest of 1066, whose only encounter with these animals would have been at the dining table. The Anglo-Saxon peasants who tended to the living beasts continued to call them by their Old English names: *cow, pig, calf, deer,* and *sheep*. This distinc- tion was first popularized by Walter Scott in his historical novel

Ivanhoe (1820), set during the reign of Richard I, where a jester explains to a peasant that 'Alderman Ox continues to hold his Saxon epithet while he is under the charge of serfs and bondsmen such as thou, but becomes Beef, a fiery French gallant, when he arrives before the worshipful jaws that are destined to consume him'. Although Scott's depiction is something of a romantic simplification— Shakespeare has Shylock compare his flesh to that of 'Muttons, Beefes, or Goates' in *The Merchant of Venice*—it does capture the extent to which the language of English cuisine is indebted to French. Given this, it is somewhat ironic that the French term for the English is *les rosbifs* 'the roast beefs'. The association of beef with the nobility is most apparent in the dubious etymology of the *sirloin*, in which a king, when served with a particularly fine piece of meat, supposedly took out his sword and knighted it 'Sir Loin'. Instead the name derives rather more prosaically from its position as the upper part (French *sur* 'above') of the loin.

But, while the French may have had nothing to do with the lowly business of tending to these animals, there is evidence that they were involved in the gruesome task of slaughtering them. Indeed, a knowledge of the correct manner of butchering an animal, and the relevant terminology, were important skills in the Middle Ages. The word *butcher* is from *buck*, the term for the male goat and deer. Professional butchers plied their trade while seated upon *shambles*; from Latin *scamnum* 'bench', this term was later transferred to the stalls on which butchers displayed their wares. In a subsequent shift, *shambles* came to refer to the slaughter house (or *abattoir*, from French *abattre* 'to beat down'), and then to any scene of *carnage* (also a meaty metaphor—from Latin *caro* 'flesh'), or, more mildly, place of disorder and mess.

In England, roasted meat is typically served with lashings of gravy, whose name probably originates in a simple scribal error. The word was originally *grané*, a French borrowing meaning 'spiced' (from Latin *granum* 'grain'). The letters u and n were often indistinguishable in medieval handwriting—both were formed using two single vertical strokes called minims—so that it would be easy for a scribe to misread the word as *graué*. While the letters 'u' and 'v' are distinguished by the sounds they represent today, in medieval English they varied according to position: 'v' appeared at the beginnings of words (*vntil* 'until') and 'u' in the middle (*loue* 'love'), irrespective of the sound. Given these differences, it is easy to see how the French word *grané* could have given rise to *gravy*. Another change in the form of a word that has arisen through *palaeographical* (Greek 'ancient handwriting') confusion is the shift from *fnesen* to modern English *sneeze*. Medieval handwriting employed several different forms of the letter 's', an 8-shaped form, another resembling a kidney bean, the Greek sigma, and a long form—still found in printed books of the eighteenth century. This last letter closely resembled the letter 'f'; it was confusion between the long 's' and 'f' that resulted in *fnesen* becoming adapted to modern English *sneeze*.

Along with meat drowned in gravy, another English favourite is the *stew*. This word derives from Greek *tuphos* 'smoke' (via the Old French form *estuve*)—the same root as *typhus*. In English the word was originally used to refer to a cauldron in which something was heated, as well as a steam room or bath. The close association of the public baths (or *stews*) with illicit activity led to the word's use to refer to a brothel. Only in the eighteenth century did the modern use of the word to refer to a slow cooked preparation consisting of meat and vegetables arise. Incidentally, the Latin word for a brothel was *fornix*—from which we get the English words *fornicate* and *fornication*. The word initially meant 'arch', the shift in meaning having been triggered by the tendency for prostitutes to hang around in archways when touting for clients. The Latin word for a prostitute was *meretrix*, which is the root of the English word *meretricious*, describing something that, while superficially attractive, has no real value or integrity.

To balance out the rather *carnivorous* (Latin *carnivorus* 'flesh-devouring') turn this discussion has taken, it is time to consider the origins of the vegetables that accompany meat dishes, or—if you are a vegetarian—replace the meat entirely. The term *vegetarian*, to describe those who abstain from meat, was coined in the mid-nineteenth century; its popularity may have been thanks to the Vegetarian Society founded in Ramsgate in 1847. *Vegan*, used of those who avoid all foods and products of animal origin, is a mid-twentieth-century coinage, based on the abbreviated form *veg*—but with a pronunciation that reflects its spelling rather than its etymology. Vegetables get their name from Latin *vegetabilis*, meaning 'animating' or 'vigorous'; despite this, it may also be used describe a state in which one is capable of only the most basic features of life. This has given rise to a number of idioms describing those in various states of inactivity, such as *couch potato* and *cabbage head*.

Vegetables

The *asparagus* takes its name from the Greek word *asparagos*; despite this simple relationship, the word's history is rather more complicated. The Greek word entered English via the medieval Latin form *sparagus*, which was subsequently anglicized into the more recognizable form *sparrow-grass*. *Sparrow-grass* was used until the nineteenth century, when it came to be considered an ignorant mistake and was replaced by *asparagus*. Also of classical origin is the *cauliflower*—ultimately from Latin *caulis* 'cabbage', which is also the source of *kale*. The word entered English via the French *chou fleuri* 'flowered cabbage'; other historical spellings, such as *collyflower*, show the partial anglicization having been taken further still.

The cucumber is straightforwardly a version of the Latin word for the same vegetable—*cucumis*; the English spelling with a 'b' reflects the influence of the medieval French form *cocombre* (compare modern French *concombre*). The Greek word for the cucumber, *angourion*, is the ultimate source of the English word for the related *gherkin*—which was borrowed into English from the Dutch word *augurkje*. As with the word *ghost* (Old English *gast*), the 'h' in *gherkin* is a later addition—the word was originally spelled without, as in Pepys's reference of 1661: 'We...opened the glass of Girkins...which are rare things.' In the seventeenth and eighteenth centuries, the pronunciation of *cucumber* as 'cow-cumber' became popular, and the word began to be spelled *cowcumber* accordingly. In the nineteenth century, this pronunciation fell out of fashion and became associated with other non-standard markers (such as aitch-dropping) as evidence of illiteracy, as in Charles Dickens's portrayal of Mrs Gamp's speech in *Martin Chuzzlewit* (1842–4): 'In case there should be such a thing as a cowcumber in the 'ouse, will you be so kind as bring it, for I'm rather partial to 'em, and they does a world of good in a sick room.' The view that cucumbers are good for your health dates back to Roman times; according to Pliny, the emperor Tiberius was advised to partake of a daily cucumber by his physicians—apparently a cucumber a day kept the doctor away. But not everyone has been persuaded by the vegetable's health benefits. Dr Johnson approvingly cited the view of English physicians that 'a cucumber should be well sliced, and dressed with pepper and vinegar, and then thrown out, as good for nothing'. Despite his enthusiasm for gherkins, Pepys would no doubt have concurred; an entry in his diary for 22 August 1663 records the demise of one Mr Newburne, who apparently died from eating 'cowcumbers'.

Salad, now used to describe a mixture of raw vegetables, was probably originally a dressing using salt, since the word derives from Latin *sal* 'salt'. A *salt-cellar* was formerly a *saler*; it was altered to *cellar* on the assumption that it was related to the word meaning 'storehouse for provisions', to which the word *salt* was added. The result is a rather *tautologous* (Greek *tautologos* 'repeating what has been said') formation, meaning 'salt salt-cellar'. The traditional placement of a salt cellar at the centre of the dining table gave rise to the expressions *above the salt* and *below the salt*, referring to seating positions of greater or lesser honour. In French the word *salade* is also used of the lettuce, alongside *laitue*, the source of the English word, going back to the Latin word *lac* 'milk'—a reference to the plant's milky juice.

From further afield is the *potato*, introduced to English from the Spanish *patata*, itself from the Caribbean word *batata* 'sweet potato'—the earliest type of potato known in England. The *avocado* is a borrowing from the Aztec language Nahuatl; the word was originally *ahuacatl*—the Nahuatl word for a testicle, so called because of its shape. Another plant that gets its name from a word for testicle is the *orchid* (Greek *orkhis*)—a name that derives from the shape of the tubers in many species—a comparison that lies behind the sixteenth-century alternatives *bollock grass* and *dog stones*.

A balanced diet (from Greek *diaita* 'way of life') also involves eating nuts and pulses. The word *nut* goes back to the Old English *hnutu*—the initial 'h' was dropped early in the word's history. The *walnut*, a particular favourite at Christmas, is from the Old English word *wealh*, meaning 'slave', or 'foreigner' (also the origin of the name of the Welsh). A walnut is thus a 'foreign nut', a name that was intended to distinguish this Italian import from the nut of the native hazel. *Almond* is ultimately a form of the Latin name for that nut, *amygdala*; the Latin word is now the medical term for an area of grey matter in each hemisphere of the brain, whose shape resembles an almond. If that seems an unlikely comparison, it's nothing compared to the *hippocampus*, which gets its name from its apparent similarity to a sea-horse (Greek *hippos* 'horse' and *kampos* 'monster'). The high-protein pulse known as the *lentil* takes its name from Latin *lenticula* 'little lens'—*lens* being the Latin word for a lentil. This word is also the root of the English word *lens*, a seventeenth-century borrowing used to refer to a curved piece of glass, on account of the similarity of its shape to that of a lentil.

If you want to boost your brainpower then seafood is the ideal choice—although in England the potential health benefits are mitigated by coating it with batter and deep-frying it. Fish is usually accompanied by *potato chips*, also known as *chips* or *French fries*. These may be soaked in *vinegar*, whose name is from the Old French *vyn egre* 'sour wine'. *Egre* is derived from Latin *acer*, also found in the English words *acerbic*, something that is 'sour tasting', and *acrid* 'bitter'. Vinegar is also an ingredient of *ketchup*, now chiefly made from tomatoes, but originally an Asian fish sauce known in Chinese as *ke-chiap*. *Ketchup* is first recorded in English in the seventeenth century, alongside variants such as *catchup, katchop, kitchup, ketsup,* and *catsup*—the last of these is now commonly used in the USA. As an alternative you might prefer *mayonnaise*, whose name may be derived from Port Mahon, the capital of Menorca, captured by the French in 1756. But other explanations have been suggested, including a corruption of *bayonnaise* (after the French town Bayonne), and a derivation from the French verb *manier* 'to handle'.

For a more upmarket seafood experience you might choose to try a shellfish or *crustacean* (from Latin *crusta* 'shell'—the same word is used for the crust on a loaf of bread). These include the *lobster*, which is etymologically related to the much less tasty and considerably less filling *locust*—both go back to Latin *locusta*. Despite its name, the *crayfish* is also a crustacean; its name is an anglicization of the Old French *crevice*, with the second element reflecting a popular assumption that an animal that lives in water must be a type of fish. The Greek word for shell, *ostrakon*, lies behind the name of the *oyster* (Greek *ostreon*). *Ostrakon* is also the root of *ostracize*, the term for excluding somebody from a group. This is because Athenians used to write the names of people they wished to see expelled from the city on a tile, or piece of pottery known as an *ostrakon*; Athenians who were exiled using this method were said to have been ostracized.

CHAPTER 13

Eating out

If you are going out to eat, you could choose to go to an Italian restaurant and enjoy the delights of pizza and pasta. The word *pizza* is of uncertain origin; it was used in Latin to refer to a flat bread topped with cheese and is perhaps related to the Germanic word *bizzo* 'bite, cake'. Less likely is the suggestion that it is connected to the Greek *plakous* 'flat cake', which is the origin of *placenta*. The *margherita* pizza is named for Margherita Teresa Giovanna of Savoy, who was Queen of Italy from 1878 to 1900. It was designed in 1889 by a Neapolitan pizza-maker named Raffaele Esposito in celebration of a visit by the Queen. The toppings of cheese, tomato, and basil were chosen to represent the white, red, and green of the Italian flag. For additional toppings you could choose from *funghi* 'mushrooms', *prosciutto* 'cured ham' (from Latin *exsuctus* 'sucked out'— referring to the drying process), or *pepperoni*, a sausage seasoned with peppers.

The word *pasta* is from an Italian word meaning 'paste', which goes back to Greek *pastai* 'barley porridge'; this is the same root that lies behind the English words *pasty*, *paste*, *patty*, *pastel*, and *pate*. The Italian word *pasticcio*, referring to a pie consisting of a mixture of pasta and meat, was borrowed into English to refer to a musical or written work featuring contributions by a variety of composers or writers. From this developed the sense of a work deliberately created in order to imitate the style of another, and subsequently the humorous exaggeration or parody of an artist with which the word's modern descendant, *pastiche*, is associated. Pasta cooked so that it is still firm when bitten is termed *al dente*, literally 'to the tooth'.

Pasta

The various types of pasta usually take their names from their appearance. *Fusilli* derives from a regional word meaning 'little spindles', referring to their twisting or spiral shape. *Conchiglie* means 'conch shells', again referencing their shape; the Latin *concha* 'bivalve shell' that lies behind this word is also the root of English *conch*, now used for a wider variety of mollusc shells. *Spaghetti* is the diminutive of *spago* 'string', hence 'little strings', while *vermicelli* means 'little worms', from Latin *vermis* 'worm'— also the root of *vermin*. *Cannelloni* means 'large stalks', *tagliatelle*, pasta cut into ribbons, is from *tagliare* 'to cut', while *fettuccine* means 'little ribbons'. *Penne* pasta, in the form of hollow tubes with a diagonal cut at each end, is so called because of its resemblance to a feather or a quill pen. *Farfalle*, bow-shaped pieces of pasta, take their name from the Italian word for a butterfly or a bow tie—*farfalla*. *Pappardelle*, pasta shaped as flat, broad ribbons, is from Italian *pappare* 'to eat hungrily'.

Macaroni is from the Greek *makaria* 'food made from barley'. In the eighteenth century it came to be used of a dandy or a fop: a young man who, having travelled Europe, returned arrayed in extravagant European fashions of dress—men like Yankee Doodle of the famous song, who 'put a feather in his cap and called it Macaroni'. The connection between *macaroni* and a fop appears to be the Macaronic Club, a gentlemen's dining club specializing in foreign dishes. Drawing on the sense of a jumble or medley, *macaronic* came to be applied to a burlesque verse form in which Latin endings and structures were mixed with a vernacular language.

The flat sheets of pasta called *lasagne* take their name from the Latin *lasanum* 'chamber pot', presumably with reference to the vessel in which the dish was traditionally cooked. Many dishes have acquired their names in such a manner; the *casserole* gets its title from the French *casse* 'spoon-like container'. The Spanish *paella* goes back to the Latin *patella* 'small dish'—a reference to the distinctive shallow container in which the mixture of rice, chicken, seafood, and vegetables is cooked. This word is also the source of the medical term for the kneecap, so called because it too resembles a small dish. In the case of Spanish *tapas*, it is the manner in which they are served rather than cooked that gives them their name. *Tapas* means 'lids', referring to the way that these small dishes of savoury nibbles offered in bars (or *bodegas*) were originally served on a small dish balanced on the top of a glass.

Italian pasta dishes are typically served with a sauce; pasta *alla carbonara*, for example, means in the carbonara style (*alla* 'in the style of'). *Carbonara* itself is of uncertain etymology; it may be the name of a restaurant that originally served the dish, or a regional word for a charcoal burner, *carbonaro*, from Latin *carbo* 'charcoal'—the source of English *carbon*. While *bolognese* sauce can be linked straightforwardly with the northern Italian city of Bologna, the spicy sauce known as *arrabbiata* gets its name from the verb *arrabbiare* 'to get angry' or 'to catch rabies', from Latin *rabbia*—the source of the English words *rabies* and *rage*. The tomato sauce flavoured with olives, capers, and anchovies known as *puttanesca* is from the Italian *puttana* 'prostitute'. The reason behind this name is unclear, although one suggestion is that it was invented by prostitutes because it could be prepared quickly between visiting clients. The thin strips of meat known as *carpaccio* are named for a

Venetian painter called Vittore Carpaccio (c.1460–1525), who used a red pigment that resembled raw meat. The dish itself was first devised in Venice in the 1960s, when Carpaccio's work was on exhibition at the Doge's Palace.

Another popular option for dining out is the Indian restaurant, or curry house, where you can enjoy the delicious tastes and *aromas* (from Greek *aroma* 'spice') of Asian cookery. English *curry* is from the Tamil *kari*, the name given to a spicy sauce. While treating someone to an Indian meal is certain to put you in their good books, this is not the origin of the phrase *currying favour*. This idiom derives from the Old French *correier* 'to prepare, arrange', which was originally used to refer to a process of grooming using a comb, but which later took on the sense of using flattery to win favour. The phrase *to curry favour* was originally *currying favel—favel* being a stock name for a pale brown (or *fallow*) horse; from describing someone grooming a horse, the phrase came to refer to someone employing flattery to attempt to win personal advantage.

Curry

Perhaps the easiest curry name to explain is that of the hot sauce known as the *madras*, which is named after the Eastern seaport of Madras, known today as Chennai. Of less exotic origins is the *balti*, which was invented in Birmingham in the 1980s. But despite its local and recent origins, the origin of its name remains unclear. Since the dish is typically served in a round-bottomed metal pan it is often thought to derive from the Hindi word *bālṭī* 'bucket', but there is no evidence of the Hindi word being used to describe the curry dish. Another possible source is the Panjabi word *bāṭṭī*, used of a brass dish of similar proportions, but how this word could have changed to *balti* is not clear. *Tandoori* is used of meat cooked in a clay oven in northern India or Pakistan, from Urdu *tandūr* 'oven', while *biryani* is from a Hindi word meaning 'fried' or 'roasted'. The *rogan josh* gets its name from the Urdu words for oil and stew—somehow 'oily stew' doesn't sound quite as appetizing.

Curries whose names reflect their core ingredients include the *dopiaza*—from Urdu *dopiyāza*, meaning 'two onions', since this ingredient is added twice during the cooking process. The spicy sauce known as the *vindaloo* gets its name from the Portuguese words for its major ingredients: *vinho* 'wine' and *alho* 'garlic'. Less helpful in identifying the constituent ingredients is the term *jalfrezi*, which is from a Bengali word simply meaning 'spicy food'. Similarly vague is the *korma*, from Turkish *kavurma* 'cooked meat'; even less specific is the *masala*, which is from the Urdu word *maṣālā*, meaning 'ingredients'. The *pasanda* gets its name from the Persian word *pasand*, meaning 'excellent', which does at least suggest that—whatever it may contain—it should at least taste nice. Curry is often eaten with rice; originating in the Greek *oruza*, this word entered English from Old French *ris*. The French word is a borrowing of the Italian *riso*, from which we get *risotto*. *Naan bread* is something of a tautology—since *naan* is the Urdu word for 'bread'. An essential accompaniment is the *poppadom*, a borrowing of the Tamil word *pappatam*; but, while it features on all Indian menus, there is little agreement on how the word should be spelled—*poppadum, popadom, popadum*, and even *puppadom* all make regular appearances.

Whatever you decide to eat, you will undoubtedly wish to finish off with something sweet. But, once you know that the word *pudding* is from Anglo-Norman *bodeyn* 'sausage', which in turn appears to derive from Latin *botellus* 'small intestine', you may find yourself suddenly feeling unexpectedly full. The connection between the sweet desserts that we eat today and sausages is the bag or casing in which they were both cooked. The word *pudding* was originally used to refer to both sweet and savoury dishes cooked in this manner, as it still is with steak and kidney and Christmas puddings.

The word *dessert* derives from the French verb *desservir*, literally meaning 'to de-serve', i.e. 'to clear the table'; it was initially used to describe a course comprising fruits and sweetmeats served after the table had been cleared. This usage continues today in Oxbridge colleges, much to the surprise of guests who, having consumed a pudding course, find themselves being invited to *take dessert*. Another term often used to refer to this course is *sweet*, but the fortunes of this word suffered at the hands of Nancy Mitford and the U and non-U debate—as captured in John Betjeman's satirical poem *How to Get On in Society* (1951): 'Is trifle sufficient for sweet?' Branded the non-U equivalent of the correct term *pudding*, *sweet* lives on in some dialects, but is more usually heard with reference to children's confectionery. Also of restricted currency but still in use are *afters*, and *seconds*—though the latter is more commonly used to refer to a second helping of any course. Technically speaking, therefore, one can have seconds of afters. The proof, as they say, is in the pudding. If you're wondering how the proof of anything can be located in a sweet dessert, the reason for your confusion is that our modern version of this proverb is a corruption of the original form, first recorded in 1605 as *the proof of the pudding is in the eating*. A further cause of uncertainty is that the word *proof* is being used in its older sense of 'test'—preserved today in a *proofreader* who checks the test pages (or *proof*) of a book before publication. Confusion has been further encouraged by the tendency for people to use a shortened version of the proverb—*the proof of the pudding*. Since the word *proof* is today more commonly used to mean 'evidence', the phrase was reworded as if it implied that the evidence for some claim can be located in a pudding. The true explanation of this phrase is quite simple—especially for fans of the *Great British Bake-Off* TV Show—it doesn't matter how fancy the decoration and presentation, the true test of a pudding is in how it tastes. Or, more generally, the success of something can only be judged by putting it to its intended use.

Puddings

Eponymous puddings include the *pavlova*, a dessert made of meringue, whipped cream, and fruit, named after the Russian ballerina Anna Pavlova (1881–1931). Despite its Russian associations, it was actually invented in Australia and New Zealand and named after the star following her 1926 tour of the Antipodes (referring to those living on the opposite side of the world—from Greek *antipodes* 'having the feet opposite'). The *tarte Tatin*, a puff pastry filled with apple, takes its name from two sisters, Stéphanie and Caroline Tatin, who invented it at their French hotel.

The *trifle*, a sponge cake covered in custard, jelly, and cream, gets its name from a word originally adopted in English from Old French *truffler* 'to mock, deceive', and used to mean 'a story designed to deceive'. The *fool* gets its name from the word for a simpleton; its origins lie in the Latin word for 'bellows', *follis*, which was later extended to refer to a 'windbag' or 'idiot'. The use of this word to refer to the dessert was probably suggested by the related *trifle*. Another dessert whose name refers to the process of inflating is *soufflé*, a light sponge dish, from a French word meaning 'blown'. Similarly, *puff pastry* (formerly *puff paste*) gets its name from the lightness of this flaky pastry being like a puff of wind.

The English favourite *treacle tart* goes back to Greek *theriake*, via the French word *triacle*. The Greek word referred to an antidote used to combat animal venom (from *therion* 'wild beast'); its earliest senses in English refer to a medicine used against poisonous bites and other unpleasant infections and diseases. The use of *treacle* as an alternative to the more usual English translation *balm* in certain translations of the Bible, as in Jeremiah 8:22 'Is there no balm in Gilead?', led to the coining of the nickname *Treacle Bible*. Traditionally treacle tart is eaten with custard. The word for this gloopy, yellow sauce, made of milk and eggs, was originally *crustarde*, a term which was used to denote an open pie containing meat or fruit with a thick sauce. The origins of *crustarde* are shared with modern English *crust* and refer to the dish's hard casing; both words go back to Latin *crusta* 'hard shell, rind'.

The *pie*, which may be either savoury or sweet, is from the same source as the second element of *magpie*. The connection between the avian pie and the edible variety seems to have been the similarity between the bird's propensity to collect random objects and the way that a pie comprises a collection of varied ingredients. A pudding that originated as a savoury dish is *blancmange*—from French *blanc* 'white' and *manger* 'to eat'—initially a dish of minced meat in a white sauce made of cream and eggs. The name of the French dessert *croquembouche* describes its texture rather than its appearance; originating in the French *croque-en-bouche*, the name means 'that is crunched in the mouth' (from *croquer* 'to bite' and *bouche* 'mouth'). The Italian dessert known as *panna cotta* describes the method of production, as it derives from the Italian for 'cooked cream'—which, unfortunately, is unlikely to turn into *crème brûlée* (French for 'burned cream') if you overcook it. Rather more inventive is *tiramisu*, from the Italian for 'pick me up'; a similar idea lies behind the name of the veal dish *saltimbocca*, which literally means 'leap into the mouth'. The prize for the most unpromising pudding name must surely go to *tapioca*, which is from the name used by the Tupi, a South American people, *tipioca*, from *tipi* 'dregs' and *ok* 'squeeze out'.

PART IV

Sport & Leisure

CHAPTER 14

Sports

After a busy day it is now time to unwind, which for many involves participating in some form of sporting contest. Although today *sport* typically refers to an organized game with a competitive element, the word itself is a shortened form of *disport*, from Latin *dis* 'away' and *portare* 'to carry', reflecting an earlier use to refer to any kind of entertainment that takes you out of yourself. It was in the nineteenth century that our modern use of the word to refer to formal competitions requiring skill and physical exertion was introduced, initially with reference to blood sports and field sports, such as hunting, shooting, and fishing. If your definition of sport is one that places stress on the physical exertion, preferably with a little bloodshed thrown in, then the game for you is rugby.

Rugby

Originally known as *rugby-football*, to distinguish it from its ancestor *association football*, the game of *rugby* is named after Rugby School (in the Warwickshire town of Rugby) where the sport was invented in the nineteenth century. The abbreviated form *rugger* was also coined at the school, by adding the '-er' suffix common to much public school and Oxbridge slang (like *footer* or *soccer* for *football*, or *brekker* for *breakfast*). Students at Oxford University still compete for a trophy or cup in intercollegiate *cuppers* sporting tournaments.

In a game of rugby each team has fifteen players, divided into *forwards* and *backs*. The forwards make up the *pack* or *scrum* (an abbreviated form of *scrummage*). Although a *set-scrum* is officially described as an 'orderly formation of players used to restart play', it is often a good deal more chaotic, reflecting its roots in a variant form of the noun *skirmish* 'an episode of irregular or unpremeditated fighting' between armies or fleets of ships. More informal scrums created during open play are called *mauls* (from a medieval term for striking someone with a heavy weapon, originally Latin *malleus* 'hammer') or *rucks* (from a Scandinavian word for a heap or stack— related to *rick* 'haystack'). The technical difference between the two is whether the ball is in the hand or on the ground—a distinction that can be difficult to apply when lying underneath a heap of bodies and being trampled on by studded boots.

The front row is made up of a *hooker* (so called because his job is to hook the ball out of the back of the scrum), supported by two *props*. Behind them are the *second row* (or *locks*), while the *back row* (originally used of a chorus line of dancers) consists of two *flankers* (from the term used for the outer edges of an army) and a *number eight*. The forwards' job is to *outshove* the opponent's pack so as to deliver the ball to the *backs*, or *three-quarters*: the *scrum-half*, *fly-half*, *wingers*, and *full-back*. These positions were originally termed *half-backs* or *quarter-backs*—the latter is now a key role in an American football team.

The aim of the game is to touch the ball down over the opponents' *goal-line*, thereby scoring a *try*—so called because it wins the right to try to *kick a goal*. A try was originally known as a *touchdown*, another rugby term that is better known for its use in American football (although ironically there is no requirement to touch the ball on the ground). *Kicking a goal*, or *converting a try* (once known quaintly as *majorizing*), is achieved by kicking the ball through the upright posts.

A distinctive feature of rugby is that the ball can only be passed backwards. As well as the *forward pass*, players should avoid the *hospital pass*—where the ball is offloaded to a team mate just as a burly opponent prepares to make a crunching tackle. The name derives from the likelihood of the recipient requiring hospital treatment. There are various types of tackle: some—like the *ankle tap*—sound quite gentlemanly, while others—the *choke, crash, dump, smother*, and *spear tackles*, decidedly more brutal. The *late tackle* (carried out after the ball has been passed) is really a euphemism for an attack on an opponent without the ball. Given the rather physical nature of the game, it is perhaps not surprising to find players getting injured, or what rugby players themselves refer to dismissively as *getting a knock*. A *blood injury* requires a player to leave the field in order to receive treatment (generally in the form of the *magic sponge*, a sponge soaked in cold water which appears to cure all ailments) in the *blood bin* (not to be confused with the *sin bin* to which a player goes following a yellow card).

Instead of passing, a player may opt to kick the ball using one of several methods: the *drop-kick* (when the ball is kicked as it hits the ground), *punt* (kicked before hitting the ground, from a dialect word meaning 'push forcefully'), *place-kick, up-and-under* (also known as the *Garryowen* after an Irish rugby club in Limerick), or *grub-kick* or *grubber* (which runs along the ground). Less orthodox is the *hack* (from an Old English word meaning 'cut in pieces')—an intentional kicking of an opponent's shins instead of the ball. This should not be confused with the *haka*, a ceremonial Maori war dance that is performed by the New Zealand All Blacks before every match. If this description of the game has not already put you off, there is no sight more guaranteed to make you glad that you are watching from the safety of the stands than fifteen huge Kiwis performing this intimidating display.

If this hasn't satisfied your desire for physical sporting contests you might try your hand (or fist) at boxing, or *pugilism*—from Latin *pugil* 'boxer', related to *pugnus* 'fist', from which we get the English word *pugnacious* 'quarrelsome, belligerent'. The central objective of boxing is fairly self-explanatory—felling your opponent so that they *kiss the canvas*; to win you must knock them *out for the count*—with reference to the counting of ten seconds by the referee. If a boxer gets back to his feet before the count is complete, he is said to *come up smiling*—the origin of a phrase describing any attempt to put a brave face on a taxing situation. If he instead fails to return to his feet, his opponent is declared the winner by having his arm raised, also known as *getting the duke* (from the boxing slang term *duke* for the hand). In boxing the aim is to deliver a series of *body blows*—forceful punches to the torso, now used metaphorically of any major disappointment. Other legitimate attempts are named after the area of the body at which they are aimed, such as the *mugger* or *muzzler*, a punch on the face, *nobber*, a blow to the head, and the self-explanatory *ribber* and *throater*; a knockout blow is known as an *outer*. The *peekaboo*, better known as a game to entertain young children, is decidedly more sinister in its boxing incarnation, since it describes a sudden punch delivered after a period of defence, in which the gloves are held up to cover the face.

From this account it might sound as if anything goes, but in reality boxing contests follow the rules that were set down under the *aegis* (a Greek term for the shield of Zeus) of Sir John Sholto Douglas, 8th Marquis of Queensberry, in 1867. Known as the *Marquis of Queensberry rules*, this phrase has been extended to encompass any rules of gentlemanly conduct and etiquette. These include the prohibition on hitting your opponent in the genitals—euphemistically referred to as *punching below the belt*—which has come to refer to any kind of unsportsmanlike conduct. Also illegal is the *rabbit punch*, a blow to the back of the head, named after its use to kill rabbits. Also originating in the boxing ring is the expression *punching above one's weight*—referring to someone who exercises more influence than their status would suggest.

A boxer who is under pressure from his opponent may find himself forced back onto the ropes surrounding the ring; from this we get the expression *on the ropes*, referring to any challenging situation where defeat seems inevitable. To be *on the back foot*, now used of any disadvantageous position, originated in a defensive stance adopted by a boxer. In such situations one might be tempted to *throw in the towel* and accept defeat, another boxing idiom, that originated in the practice of throwing a towel into the ring to signal submission; in the nineteenth century it was a sponge that was used, hence the less common alternative *chuck up the sponge*.

For a less violent way of indulging in a sporting contest, you might prefer to try your hand at cricket. With its long history and central place in English sporting culture, it is hardly surprising that cricketing idioms have been widely adopted into colloquial speech. The traditional association of cricket with fair play and good sportsmanship has given rise to expressions such as *play with a straight bat*, meaning 'behave honestly and decently', and *it's just not cricket*, to refer to any behaviour that flouts common standards of decency and fairness. The origins of other commonly used cricketing idioms are less obvious. Someone who has lived to a ripe old age is said to have enjoyed a *good innings*, a phrase which compares long life to a successful period spent at the crease. To do something *off your own bat*, or on your own initiative, can also be traced to the cricket pitch. Since this is often mistakenly corrupted to *off your own back*, the phrase's cricketing connections are evidently not widely known.

Cricket

In cricket a ball is *bowled*, a usage which recalls the original practice of rolling the ball along the ground, as with carpet bowls. This form of underarm bowling was replaced by the technique of *round-arm* or *round-hand* delivery; this subsequently developed into the *over-hand* or *over-arm* style of bowling employed today. The rich variety of bowling styles has produced a collection of exotic terms. The gentlest deliveries are the *full toss* (which travels to the batsman without bouncing), *donkey drop* (describing its high, looping arc), *grubber* (which travels along the ground, like a grub), and *daisy-cutter* (another term for a ball that skims the ground, beheading daisies along the way). Considerably more taxing for the batsman are the *flipper, slider, googly, chinaman, yorker*, and *doosra*. The origins of these terms are a testimony to the game's global popularity, especially in Britain and its former colonies; *yorker* is named after the city of York, *doosra* is derived from the Hindi word *dūsrā* 'second, other' (coined by Pakistani wicketkeeper Moin Khan when he encouraged bowler Saqlain Mushtaq to 'bowl the other one'), while *chinaman* is named after Ellis Achong, a West Indian bowler of Chinese descent.

Batting terms are more plainly descriptive, including *cut, cover drive, sweep*, and *hook*, although less regulation shots tend to attract more unusual names, such as the *cow-shot* (in which the ball is pulled towards *cow-corner*), and the *agricultural shot* (using a scything motion which uproots a generous quantity of turf). Hitting the ball over the boundary earns the batsman four runs; if the ball crosses the boundary without bouncing, six runs are awarded. This is the origin of the expression *hit for six*, describing a feeling of overwhelming surprise. A batsman who fails to score is said to have received a *duck*, an abbreviation of *duck's egg*. This is a reference to the resemblance of the number 0 to a duck's egg; the same link has been proposed for the use of *love* to refer to a score of zero in tennis. According to this theory, *love* is a corruption of the French word for an egg, *l'oeuf*; more likely is a connection with the phrase *playing for love*, rather than for money. Failure to score any runs in a period of six balls, known as an *over*, is termed a *maiden*, drawing on an archaic use of the word to mean 'virgin' (as in *maidenhood*).

There are many ways for a batsman to be *dismissed, out*, or *lose his wicket*: *caught, bowled, leg-before-wicket, hit-wicket, run out*, and *stumped*—the last of these is now widely used to describe facing any impasse, or problem, for which no solution presents itself. Another cricketing term referring to a tricky situation is *sticky wicket*, used of a wet pitch which has not fully dried, and consequently prone to unpredictable bounces. The end of the game is marked by the *drawing of stumps*, indicating *close of play*, another cricketing idiom that has been drawn into general use, especially to refer to the end of the working day.

If you don't have the full six hours required for the average cricket match, perhaps the mere four hours demanded for a game of golf would suit you better. If so, it's time to take a trip to the nearby golf course, or *links*—from the Old English *hlinc* 'rising ground, ridge'; in Scottish use this word came to be used specifically of undulating ground near seashore, and from this derived the golfing sense of a course located near the sea.

Golf

In a game of golf, competitors will be aiming to make *par*—the standard number of shots allowed for each hole (from the Latin for 'equal')—hence the expression *par for the course*. Scoring below par results in a *birdie*, a word which originates in an American slang term for an impressive achievement. A more literal interpretation of *birdie*, originating in a story of a golfer who managed to score below par on a hole despite hitting a bird with his opening drive, has given rise to the terms *eagle* (two under par) and *albatross* (three under par). A score above par is known as a *bogey*; originally the term for the 'ground score', the expected number of shots per hole, its origin is thought to derive from a Major Wellman, who likened playing against the ground score to competing with a 'regular bogey-man'.

The modern game of golf has dropped many of the wonderfully quaint terms for clubs in favour of a bland numbering system. Sadly, golfers no longer brandish the *niblick* (or 'little beak'), *brassy* (coated in brass), *baffy* (from French *baffe* 'blow with the back of the hand'), *mashie* (from French *masse* 'sledgehammer'), or *jigger* (apparently related to the dance) wielded by the game's early practitioners. If you want to get a flavour of the lost language of golf, try reading P. G. Wodehouse's golf stories, narrated by the jaded ex-player known only as the Oldest Member. Another anti-quated golf term is the verb *foozle*, meaning 'mess up' or 'bungle' a shot; appropriately enough, this verb can also be used to mean 'fool around' or 'waste time'. Although they no longer *foozle*, modern golfers are just as likely to *hook, slice, top,* or *shank* a shot; most embarrassing of all is the *whiff*—or air shot—although at least there is no difficulty locating the ball afterwards. For the amateur golfer, there's something comforting about watching a professional reduced to shouting *fore*—a warning to those standing before (hence *'fore*) the ball, which follows a stray shot. Professional golfers, however, are unlikely to be offered a *mulligan*: the chance to replay the shot without having it count on the scorecard. The term was coined by David B. Mulligan (1871–1954), a keen golfer (and presumably an erratic driver), who introduced it to the Winged Foot Golf Club in New York State.

But while golf has a major global following—especially when Tiger Woods is involved—the most popular British sport is undoubtedly football. Football is less widely played in the USA, where it is known as *soccer*—an abbreviation of *Association Football*—to distinguish the game from *football*, what the Brits call *American football*. Unlike rugby and American football, here the aim of the game is to kick the ball into (rather than over) the *goal*—the term for the structure made up of wooden uprights joined by a crossbar, originating in a word for a boundary or limit. From this sense has derived the metaphorical sense of *goal* to mean an outcome to which a particular effort is directed.

Football

In the world of professional football, teams are picked by their managers, although there are now a variety of names for this position, such as Coach or Director of Football, reflecting the complex politics and hierarchies of individual clubs. Such titles are rarely observed by the players themselves, who usually stick to more informal monikers such as *gaffer* (a contraction of *godfather*, originally employed as a term of respect for an old man) and *boss* (from the Dutch *baas* 'master', or formerly 'uncle'). In a determination to foster an alternative, player-led culture in the England camp, newly appointed English boss Gareth Southgate broke with this tradition and instructed the players to call him by his first name. Teams are made up of *attackers, midfielders, defenders, wingers*, and a *goalkeeper* (also known as the *keeper*, or *goalie*)—names that describe the designated roles. In the modern game, however, there is considerably more variation in the roles and positions adopted—especially by the top players. Hence *full-backs* can often be seen tearing forward to take up attacking positions, while a *false nine* is a centre forward who drops back into the midfield in order to cause confusion for the opponent's marking system. Formations are generally described using numbers, such as 4-5-1, comprising 4 defenders, 5 midfielders, and a *lone striker*; rather more poetically, the formation 4-3-2-1 is known as the *Christmas Tree*. Even with all these strategic and tactical advances, there still remains a place for the old-fashioned *route one*: hoofing the ball over the entire pitch in the hope of reaching the *centre-forward*. Marking can take on various forms—*zonal marking*, where each player is responsible for an area of the pitch, or *man-marking*, which means pursuing a single individual all over the ground. The ultimate defensive strategy—where all 11 players are given defensive duties—is known as *parking the bus*, a term coined by José Mourinho, one of its finest exponents.

In addition to the players selected for the *starting eleven*, the *squad* comprises a number of substitutes who occupy the *bench* or the *dugout*—a term that was used in the Second World War to refer to an air raid shelter. As well as occupying a seat in the dugout, the manager can make use of a *technical area*—a small patch of grass marked out with white chalk from which he can bellow furious instructions at his players. The opposition manager's technical area is just close enough to allow the exchange of insults, but not sufficiently close to permit the exchange of fisticuffs—known in footballing circles as *handbags*.

Various match officials ensure that the rules of the game are enforced, both on and off the pitch. In overall charge is the *referee*—so called because they are the people to whom matters of dispute are referred for a decision. Referees are assisted by *linesmen*—who judge when a ball has gone out of play, when a player is offside, and help the referee identify instances of foul play. The committing of a foul leads to the awarding of a *free kick*, or a *penalty*—from French *pénalité* 'punishment, suffering', ultimately derived from the same Latin root that gives us modern English *penal*. Referees can further punish particularly dangerous or cynical fouls (ones where a player makes no attempt to play the ball—also known by the more euphemistic name *professional fouls*) by awarding the offender a *yellow card*—two of which result in a *red card*, leading to the player being *sent off*, *dismissed*, or *taking an early bath*. Particularly unpleasant fouls can result in the highest form of punishment—the *straight red*—where a player is sent off without having first received a yellow card. This is almost certainly followed by the player in question expressing the full gamut of emotions from outraged innocence through amazement, consternation, befuddlement, disgust, anger, and finally reluctant acceptance.

The referee is also responsible for ensuring the game lasts the full ninety minutes, adding any extra time to allow for stoppages; *Fergie time*—named after the Manchester United manager Sir Alex Ferguson—was coined by opposition fans to refer to the excessive periods of stoppage time that appeared to be played when his team were in search of an *equalizer* or *late winner*. Alex Ferguson is himself responsible for coining a term that has become widely used—*squeaky bum time*—referring to the anxious final stages of a league season. Famous footballers have left their mark on the game's lexicon in various ways. The *Cruyff turn* is named after the Dutch legend Johan Cruyff, the *Panenka*—a penalty where the ball is delicately chipped over the goalkeeper—after Antonín Panenka, who scored using this method in the final of the 1976 UEFA European Championship. *The Hand of God* is the name given to the goal scored by Argentinian Diego Maradona using his hand against England in the quarter-finals of the 1986 World Cup. When questioned about the legitimacy of the goal in the subsequent press conference, Maradona claimed that the goal was scored 'a little with the head of Maradona and a little with the hand of God'.

The origins of the names of football clubs are fairly self-explanatory, since many are named after the city in which they play: Manchester City, Southampton, Liverpool. But there are exceptions, such as Arsenal, named after the Royal Arsenal in Woolwich, whose workers formed the club in 1886. The Royal Arsenal was an armaments factory and storehouse; its name is ultimately of Arabic origin, meaning 'house of industry'. When the club moved from southeast London to Highbury in 1913, it dropped the word Woolwich from its name and became Arsenal Football Club.

Like Arsenal, many clubs are simply named *Football Club*; common variants include *City, Town*, and *United*. While *United* now conjures up a sense of the players serving together towards a common goal, it was originally adopted for more prosaic reasons by teams formed by merging together several existing clubs. The names *Wanderers*, as in Wolverhampton and Dundee, and *Rovers*, as in Bristol and Raith, were adopted by teams without a permanent home ground. Not all football clubs follow these established patterns. *Tottenham Hotspur* takes its second name from a medieval word used to describe a rash and impetuous person, a metaphoric use of a term which literally refers to someone whose riding spurs are hot from fast and frequent riding. The name *Albion*, adopted by West Bromwich, Brighton & Hove, and Burton, is an ancient term for Britain. It derives from the Latin word *albus* 'white', a reference to the white cliffs of Dover. The origins of Sheffield Wednesday go back to its earliest history as a cricket club; the club took the name *Wednesday* for the simple reason that it was the day when they played their matches.

The most common nicknames refer to a club's shirt colour—*The Reds, The Blues*—or its associations. Particularly popular are comparisons with the markings of animals (Hull *Tigers*), insects (Watford *Hornets*), or birds (Newcastle United *Magpies*). Norwich City's nickname, *The Canaries*, appears to have the same origin, given its bright yellow strip. But the name actually derives from the popularity of canary breeding in the city that stretches back to the Middle Ages, when the bird was imported by weavers from the Low Countries. As well as adopting the bird's colours for their strip, the club placed a canary on its badge. Sheffield Wednesday's avian nickname, *The Owls*, is nothing to do with the club's colours or with the popularity of owls in South Yorkshire; it was coined because their Hillsborough stadium is situated in the Owlerton district of the city.

Other nicknames recall local industrial associations; Arsenal's sobriquet, *The Gunners*, is a further reference to its beginnings in an armaments factory. A similar origin lies behind West Ham F.C.'s moniker, *The Hammers*, which has nothing to do with the club's name; instead it marks its foundation by members of the Thames Ironworks, further signalled by the crossed hammers on the club's badge. Sunderland A.F.C. are known as *The Black Cats* after a gun battery on the River Wear, so called because workers repeatedly reported hearing the miaowing of a mysterious black cat. The Liverpool club Everton—originally known as *St Domingo's*—is known as *The Toffees*, from Mother Noblett's Toffee Shop which was frequented by fans before matches. This gave rise to the tradition of the Toffee Lady who distributes sweets to fans before home games. The Scottish club Celtic F.C. was originally formed for the immigrant Irish population of Glasgow's East End. The club's Irish roots are marked both by its official name Celtic (pronounced unusually with a soft 's' rather than the more usual hard 'k') and the spelling of its nickname, *The Bhoys*, whose 'bh' imitates the spelling practices of the Gaelic language.

While many football stadiums are named after their locations, others have names linked to their local heritage. The home of Sunderland F.C. is known as *The Stadium of Light*, a tribute to the club's connection with the mining industry; a monument to the Davy lamp stands at the stadium's entrance. Although it was more commonly known as *Upton Park*, after its East London location, West Ham United's former stadium was officially termed *The Boleyn Ground*. This name dates from the original club's use of the grounds of Boleyn Castle, owned by Anne Boleyn, second wife of King Henry VIII until her beheading in 1536. Anne Boleyn's hunting grounds covered part of the area on which William Craven, 6th Baron Craven, constructed a house in 1780; when this building was destroyed by fire at the end of the nineteenth century, the land was bought by

Fulham F.C. as the site of their new stadium, still known today as *Craven Cottage*. Other names preserve an association with the land on which the stadium was constructed. The home of West Bromwich Albion was built on a site covered in hawthorn bushes, which had to be cleared to make way for the stadium now known as *The Hawthorns*. The stadium built for Bournemouth A.F.C. was situated on a cherry orchard, giving rise to the club's nickname *The Cherries*.

More recently the practice has been to name stadiums after their financial sponsors, as in *The Emirates* stadium, the new home of Arsenal. The strength of feeling that a change of an existing stadium name can provoke was apparent from the furore that broke out when the traditional home of Newcastle United, *St. James's Park*, was rebadged as the *Sports Direct Arena* by owner Mike Ashley. The original name was restored by Wonga.com when they became the club's main sponsors in 2012. Less contentious is the practice of naming individual stands after famous figures associated with the club. On his retirement in 2011, Manchester United named the North stand of its Old Trafford stadium (memorably labelled 'The Theatre of Dreams' by Sir Bobby Charlton) after its most successful manager, Sir Alex Ferguson. Jurgen Klopp's appointment as manager of Liverpool F.C. in October 2015 was a gift to journalists in search of appropriate puns (*King of the Kop*/*Kop Flop*), since his surname recalls the name of the famous stand at Anfield known as *The Kop*. The Liverpool stand was named after Spion Kop, a hill in KwaZulu-Natal, the site of a battle in the Boer War, where hundreds of local men serving in the Lancashire Regiment were killed.

If chasing a ball round a field in the cold doesn't appeal, you might prefer a racket (or *racquet*) sport—often played on a heated court and involving less physical contact and a lot less mud. The most popular racket sport today is tennis, but this is a comparatively late development of a much earlier game, known today to *aficionados* (originally a term for a bullfighting enthusiast) as *real tennis*. As well as being the king of racket sports, real tennis is a game of kings—its best-known royal exponent was Henry VIII, whose passion for the game led to the construction of numerous courts, or tennis *plays*, at royal palaces; the court he built at Hampton Court Palace in 1530 remains in use today. Henry was reputedly playing tennis when news was brought to him of the execution of Anne Boleyn. Perhaps the most famously incompetent member of the English royalty to try his hand at the game was Charles II; Samuel Pepys records watching the king play tennis in his diary for 1664: 'To the Tennis Court, and there saw the King play at tennis and others; but to see how the King's play was extolled, without any cause at all, was a loathsome sight.' These royal associations have given rise to the theory that the name *real* tennis derives from the Spanish *real* 'royal', as it does in the name of the famous Spanish football team Real Madrid. But the true explanation is simpler: *real* was adopted to identify real tennis as the genuine article, and thereby distinguish it from its newfangled offspring, known as *lawn tennis*. First devised in the late nineteenth century by Major Walter Clopton Wingfield, lawn tennis was originally named *Sphairistike*, an ancient Greek word meaning 'ball-playing'. Oddly this name never caught on; the popularity of the game itself, however, caused a major downturn in the fortunes of real tennis. There are around forty courts remaining in use today, over half of which are in Britain—the oldest surviving court in the world is located at Falkland Palace in Fife, Scotland, opened in 1539 and still in use today (although the combination of the lack of roof and the Scottish climate means it is not always playable). But there are signs of growth, especially among a younger generation of players: Radley and Wellington Colleges have recently invested in new courts. The Chicago Racquet club in the USA recently re-opened a refurbished court that was first constructed in 1922.

Tennis

The name *tennis* is probably derived from the French *tenez* 'take' or 'receive', supposedly shouted by the server to signal the beginning of a *rally* (known as a *rest* in real tennis). In France, real tennis is known as *jeu de paume* 'game of the palm', recalling its origins in a game where the ball was hit with the hand rather than a racket. This origin is also preserved in the modern word *racket*, which derives from the Arabic word *raha* 'palm of the hand'. This association is preserved in the asymmetrical shape of the real tennis racket, which resembles an outstretched hand.

Real tennis, known to Americans as *court tennis*, is played on an indoor court with four walls and a sloping roof, or *penthouse*, a survival of the game's origins in the monastic cloister. Before it became associated with luxury apartments or hotel suites, a *penthouse* was an annexe with a sloping roof attached to a main building, such as a shed or outhouse (reflecting its etymological connection with *append* and *appendix*). Since it is possible to serve from almost anywhere in the service end, a wonderfully rich array of deliveries has evolved, with names that describe the flight of the ball along the sloping roof: *giraffe, railroad, caterpillar, boomerang*, and *bobble*. The receiver occupies the *hazard* end, so called because it contains various additional obstacles which can be exploited by the server. One hazard is the *tambour*, a buttress which juts out and causes the ball to bounce unpredictably. The receiver must also defend the *grille*, originally a window covered by a grating through which the monks could communicate with members of the public. A shot striking the grille is a point to the server; another winning shot is one that sends the ball into a large gallery behind the server, known as the *dedans*, from the French word meaning 'inside'.

The scoring system is identical to lawn tennis in adopting the sexagesimal system of counting (from a Latin word meaning 'sixty'), with each point won scoring 15 (the third point is today known as 40, but this is a shortening of the earlier 45); when a player has scored 60 points, a *game* is awarded. The first player to win six games is awarded the *set*. But there is one significant difference to the scoring of lawn tennis. Where a ball bounces twice without being returned, a *chase* is called. The point at which the second bounce falls is recorded, the players then change ends so that the opponent may attempt to *beat the chase*, by hitting a shot that cannot be returned and whose second bounce is closer to the back wall than that of the chase. This is an ancient system of scoring which may derive from the uneven bounces encountered when the game was played outdoors, although it is often attributed to an overweight Henry VIII who found it increasingly difficult to cover the court. The system of chases makes real tennis a tactical game—a cross between lawn tennis and chess—offering a work-out for both body and brain. Simply keeping track of the more esoteric chases—more than a yard worse than the last gallery, or hazard better than the door—can be a mental challenge in itself.

Another popular racket sport is *squash*, so called because the soft ball is squashed when hit with the racket. Like lawn tennis, squash originates in an older form of the game: in this case *rackets*—still played today in a small number of extant courts. If real tennis is the game of kings, rackets is the game of criminals—rather than originating in royal palaces, the first games of rackets were played in eighteenth-century debtors' prisons: the King's Bench and the Fleet. On finding himself incarcerated in The Fleet, the unfortunate Mr Pickwick observes a group of people congregating at the prison's *racket-ground*, in Charles Dickens's novel *The Pickwick Papers* (1836–7). From there the game spread to public houses and taverns, and subsequently to public schools and stately homes, becoming a game for the wealthy rather than the bankrupt and destitute.

The game was initially a development of the earlier game of *fives*—in which a ball is hit against the wall using the hand—but with a racket introduced to speed up the action. This certainly had the desired effect, since in a game of rackets the ball can reach dizzying speeds. In both rackets and squash points may only be scored by the server, who is said to have *hand-in*; if the receiver wins the point, the player who is *hand-out* becomes *hand-in* and takes over the serving. A serve must make contact with the end wall above the *cut-line* (rackets) or *service line* (squash), otherwise a *fault* is called (from Latin *fallita* 'failing, falling short'). In rackets the game is played to 15 points, whereas in squash a game is awarded to the first player to score 9 points (or 11 according to US rules). As both games are played on indoor courts, the ball may strike either of the sidewalls before hitting the end-wall; this shot is known as a *boast*—from the French term *bosse*, referring to the place where the ball connects with the wall. The fast pace of the game, combined with the variety of angles at which the ball can be played, means that there are plenty of opportunities for a *let* (from a word meaning 'obstruction, hindrance')—called when a player is impeded by his opponent, and resulting in the point being replayed.

An alternative racket sport is *badminton*, previously known as *battledore and shuttlecock*—*battledore* comes from a Provençal word for a paddle-shaped bat used for washing clothes and subsequently extended to encompass similarly-shaped instruments like canoe paddles; a *shuttlecock* (or *shuttlecork*) was originally a small piece of cork fitted with feathers. The game dates back to the sixteenth century; the modern game was first played by army officers stationed in India during the *Raj* (a Hindi word meaning 'government') and subsequently became popular in English country houses. The modern name of badminton comes from the title of the country seat of the Duke of Beaufort—also the location of the Badminton horse trials.

If you are a real purist and consider the use of a racket to be a modern corruption that has detracted from the true challenge, you might prefer to literally try your hand at the game known as *fives*. Since it is played with the hand, the origin of fives would seem to lie in a reference to the five fingers. But support for this explanation is hard to find. While *fives* has indeed been used as a colloquial term for the hand—as in *a bunch of fives*, referring to a closed fist—this is not recorded until two centuries after the game was devised. An alternative proposal is that it was originally played by teams comprising five players, but there's little evidence for this either. Another suggestion draws on the fact that Eton fives, like rackets, is played up to 15 points, which can be divided up into 3 sets of 5. But since there is no evidence of points being grouped in this way, this theory is hard to support. There are several different variants of the game, named after the schools at which they originated. The court used for the Eton version is modelled on part of the college's chapel, where the game was devised by pupils waiting to enter the building. The court has three walls and a buttress, known as the *pepperbox*, jutting out into the court, mirroring the side of the chapel. In the Rugby College version of the game there are no such obstacles, the court instead resembling a smaller version of a rackets court.

If even these sporting options sound too energetic, perhaps you would be better suited to the sedater pace of a game of croquet. The game's reputation as a civilized, gentle pastime is confirmed by some of the terms used by players of the game: *tea lady, dolly rush, trundle*, and *pirie poke*. But croquet has a nastier side too, witnessed by the words used to describe the tactics employed by its more competitive exponents: *aggressive spread, crunch up, death roll*, and *worse than death*. Other more recondite terms, such as *Swiss gambit, Wharrad turn, Solomon Bisque*, and *Whichelo variation*, conjure up an image of a game of chess played in a country garden.

Croquet

The aim of croquet is to strike a ball with a mallet so as to send it through a series of hoops, also termed *wires* or *arches*. In the USA these are known as *wickets* (from the Anglo-Norman form of

French *guichet* 'gate'). A number of more subtle strokes have been devised by accomplished players, such as the *jump-stroke* or *leapfrog*, designed to cause the ball to jump up by striking it into the ground—a useful way of avoiding other balls, or getting through narrow hoops from oblique angles. A shot that causes the ball to jump several times is termed a *dambuster*, after the bouncing bomb devised by British engineer Barnes Wallis for use during the Second World War. If the ball fails to pass through the hoop and remains lodged in the jaws, it is known as a *blob*.

Instead of attempting to go through a hoop, a player may adopt the more aggressive ploy of striking his ball against that of an opponent (known as the *enemy*). Having made contact with another player's ball, a player may place his own ball alongside that of the opponent and smash it in any direction. This shot is known as a *croquet*, although it is often called a *roquet* by the uninitiated—perhaps the result of confusion in a phrase such as *take croquet*, which can be misheard as *take roquet*. Muddling up these terms is a fatal solecism and a sure way of revealing yourself to be a novice to other players. Another embarrassing blunder is to inadvertently strike another player's ball while playing a croquet, known as a *Christ off*. This term originates in 1980s Cambridge; it was coined in tribute to a hapless pair of players from Christ's College who were especially prone to this gaffe. A particularly aggressive croquet can result in the opponent's ball being sent to *Hong Kong*—beyond the boundaries of the court. More subtle is the tactic of taking an opponent's ball captive—or making it a *slave*—enabling you to play multiple consecutive croquets.

An important tactic when playing doubles is known as *peeling*: the practice of knocking your partner's ball through a hoop so as to keep the two balls together. This strategic ploy is named after Walter Hayward Peel (d. 1897), founder of the United All England Croquet Association, a leading exponent of the practice. More abstruse versions of this move have been developed, such as the Aspinall Peel, defined in such terms as to mystify all but the most devoted acolyte: 'a peel attempt which is made (generally from an acute angle) with the intention of initially jawsing the peelee. As part of the same stroke, the striker's ball continues to re-strike the peelee and complete the peel by cannoning it through the hoop.'

Once a ball has passed through all the hoops in the correct sequence, all that is required to claim the game is to *peg out* by striking the ball against the winning-peg. An alternative move is to peg out your opponent's ball, by knocking it against the winning-peg, thus causing it to be disqualified. This can be a risky strategy, as noted in this account from *Country Life*: 'He had attempted to peel black and peg it out but it had not worked, and that was life—and croquet.' Instead of pegging out immediately, a player may choose to remain in play as a *rover*, disrupting other players and generally getting in the way, in order to help one's partner. But be warned: this tactic of hindering one's opponent rather than attempting to make progress is generally frowned upon; players adopting this tactic are known as *Aunt Emmas*, and considered to be rather dull exponents of the game.

For a final sporting option involving sticks and balls and demanding a minimal amount of exercise, you might consider a frame or two of snooker. While snooker does require a degree of stamina and endurance—since you are required to spend a certain amount of time on your feet—the shots themselves are played while leaning on a table. While many top snooker players would no doubt class themselves as professional sportsmen and women, it is only recently that players have been banned from drinking and smoking during competitions.

Snooker

Snooker is a nineteenth-century development of the much older game of billiards, which dates back as far as the sixteenth century. Billiards gets its name from the French word *billard* 'cue', a diminutive form of *bille* 'stick'. Once adopted into English the word was pluralized, on the model of other games, such as *draughts* and *bowls*, giving us *billiards*, or 'little sticks'. The game of snooker is called after a Woolwich slang term for a newly recruited cadet; it was transferred to the game when an army colonel stationed in Jabalpur used it to describe the poor play of a fellow officer. Another related game is a nineteenth-century American development of billiards, in which players pot balls in order to claim the collective stake or *pool*, from which the game gets its name. This word, most commonly used today in card games, is probably related in some obscure way to the French *poule*, meaning chicken.

The aim of snooker is to use the cue ball to knock the various coloured balls into the pockets—known as *hazards* in billiards. In billiards, points are also scored for a shot in which the cue ball glances off one ball onto another. This shot was known by the French term *carambole*, also an alternative name for the game itself; although it is no longer a scoring shot, the *cannon* is still known in modern snooker. Sadly, many of the exotic terms associated with billiard shots—the *postman's knock, losing hazard, floating white*, and *long Jenny*—have not been transferred to snooker. Hitting the cushion first and connecting with another ball on the rebound is termed a *double* in snooker; in billiards this was known as a *bricole*: an ancient military catapult. Failure to connect with any ball results in a *foul shot*; if a snooker player is deemed not to have made sufficient effort to hit the ball a *miss* is called, requiring the shot to be replayed. In billiards a deliberate miss designed to leave the cue ball in the comparative safety of the baulk area is known as a *miss in baulk*. The word *baulk* derives from an Old English term for an unploughed ridge, which later developed the sense of 'obstacle'. Its use in billiards derives from this later meaning, since a player is not allowed to strike a ball that is in baulk directly. The phrase *miss in baulk* enjoyed some currency in the early twentieth century as a term for deliberately avoiding carrying out an unappealing task or seeing an unwelcome person; it is particularly associated with the novels of P. G. Wodehouse, whose hero Bertie Wooster spends much of his time trying to duck the unwelcome attentions of ferocious aunts.

When a player is unable to hit the required ball because it is covered by one or more of the other balls, he is said to be *snookered*, a term which is now commonly used to refer to any difficult situation. Failure to make a clean contact with the cue ball results in a *miscue*, now in extended use to refer to any kind of mistake or misjudgement. As well as giving us words for shunning unpleasant tasks, finding ourselves in impossible situations, and making embarrassing blunders, snooker is the origin of another term we can all relate to: the *fluke*—the name given to a shot whose happy outcome was more luck than judgement. The etymology isn't known, but it may relate to a dialectal use of *fluke* to mean 'guess'.

CHAPTER 15

Animals

For a more restful and relaxing end to the working day, you might instead prefer to spend time communing with our fellow creatures. Perhaps this is the time for playing with, chatting to, or mucking out, the family pet.

Rabbits were introduced into Britain by the Normans following the Conquest, along with the name, which can be traced back to the post-Classical Latin *rabettus*. When adopted into English, *rabbit* originally designated the young animal, while another French borrowing, *coney* (ultimately from Latin *cuniculus*), was used of the adult. Rabbits were widely hunted, leading to the concept of the *coney-catcher*—a name for a rabbit-hunter, but also used of a cheat and a confidence-trickster.

Cat derives from a late Latin loanword *cattus*, which is probably ultimately of Egyptian extraction. The Classical Latin word was *feles*, the origin of the adjective *feline*, the scientific term meaning 'cat-like'; the adjectival form of *cat*—*catty*—is a term of abuse used to describe someone who is deliberately spiteful. The fashionable lingo known as *flappers' slang* used in 1920s America coined a number of unlikely expressions involving animals to describe something of top quality— amongst the widest known are *the cat's whiskers*, *the cat's pyjamas*, and *the cat's meow*. Also still in use is *the bee's knees*—other colourful examples, such as *the monkey's eyebrows*, *the gnat's elbows*, and *the elephant's adenoids*, have sadly not survived. In the seventeenth century, something of a very high standard was said to be *enough to make a cat speak*; a variant of this appears in Dickens's novel *Nicholas Nickleby* (1838–9): 'It's enough to make a Tom cat talk French grammar.' Cats feature in numerous other expressions: to be in a tricky situation is to have *a cat in hell's chance*, which might result in us looking like *something the cat's brought in*. To give away a secret is to *let the cat out of the bag*; this phrase may originate in an attempt by a market trader to pretend that a bag containing a cat actually holds a more valuable piglet. By opening the bag the deception is revealed— a similar origin lies behind the phrase *a pig in a poke* (a word for a bag now used only in Scots), referring to goods not inspected at the time of purchase which subsequently turn out to be substandard.

Rodent, the collective term for a group of mammals with prominent incisors, is from the Latin *rodere* 'to gnaw', also the root of *corrode*. The *gerbil* gets its name from Latin *gerbillus*, the diminutive form of *gerboa*—a rodent that lives in the African desert, known today as the *jerboa*. As well as rats, mice, hamsters, and gerbils, this group includes *squirrels*, whose name means 'shadow tail', and *porcupines*, from Latin *porcus* 'pig' and *spina* 'thorn'. A folk etymological association with words like *serpentine* and *turpentine* produced the variant *porpentine*—captured for posterity by its appearance in Shakespeare's *Hamlet*, where it is used by the ghost to describe the effect a description of his torments would have on Hamlet: 'Each particular haire to stand on end like quils vpon the fretfull Porpentine.' Like the porcupine, the *hedgehog* is also named for its resemblance to a pig, a reference to its protruding snout. Hedgehogs were formerly known as *irchins*—from the French *hérisson*—this word survives into modern English as *urchin*, the name given to a child who lives on the streets.

More mysterious is why *guinea pigs* should be so called, since they bear little resemblance to a pig; it may be that the squealing sound they make was thought to recall that of a pig. Similarly mysterious is the first part of their name, since they do not originate in either Guinea or New Guinea; they are instead of South American origin. A possible explanation for their association with Guinea lies in a corruption of the name of the South American country Guyana. Alternatively, it may be that Guinea was used as a generic label for a faraway country whose name was unknown. A similar origin appears to lie behind the name of the *turkey*, a bird which—despite its name— is native to America; its French name, *dinde*, is based on an equally mistaken association with India (from *d'Inde* 'of India'). The *hamster* gets its name from a German word meaning 'corn weevil', which is also misleading since, although the animal is found throughout Europe and Asia, it is not found in Germany.

The first element of *dormouse* is connected to the French verb *dormir* 'to sleep', and refers to their tendency to spend long periods in hibernation—a reputation alluded to by Lewis Carroll in the character of the soporific dormouse at the Mad Hatter's Tea Party. The word *mouse* is a straightforward adoption of the Latin *mus*; less obvious is the connection between this Latin word and the English word *muscle*. *Muscle* is a borrowing of Latin *musculus* 'little mouse', because the shape of a flexing muscle was thought to resemble a mouse moving up and down the arm. The French word for the mouse, *souris*, is unconnected, since it is derived from Latin *sorex*, the name for the shrew; the shrew is known in French as the *musaraigne*, or 'mouse spider'. In Shakespeare's day a *shrew* was also a nagging or scolding wife—as in *The Taming of the Shrew*. The nega- tive associations of the shrew have also given rise to the adjective *shrewd*; while this now refers to someone who is intelligent and astute, it originally denoted someone considered wicked or evil.

The word *dog* is one of a number of animal names, such as *frog, hog, pig,* and *stag,* whose origins are unclear. In the case of *dog,* its Old English ancestor, *docga,* appears just once in the written record: as a gloss for the Latin word *canis.* It is found in place and personal names—as in the unfortunately titled Robertus Doggisheued 'Dog's head', and even Hugo Doggetail—suggesting that it was regarded as too colloquial for formal written usage. Its form makes it unlikely that it is of Germanic origin; the more usual term for the animal in Old English was *hund,* the origin of modern English *hound.* While *hound* has survived into modern English, it is principally used of hunting dogs, or in archaic and poetic contexts to refer to dogs more generally.

As they are proverbially man's best friend, dogs feature in numerous expressions and idioms. Some of these imply that—if they are indeed our best buddies—they don't do very well out of the deal. Think of phrases like *to lead a dog's life, to die like a dog, it's not fit for a dog, to throw it to the dogs, to go to the dogs,* and *to work like a dog.* The phrase *to keep a dog and bark yourself,* referring to the practice of employing someone to do a task but then ending up doing it yourself, makes clear the expectation that dogs were intended to work for their keep. As they got older, so their usefulness diminished—as captured in the proverb *you can't teach an old dog a new trick.* The reward for this loyal service was food and lodging, but since the phrase *dog's dinner*—as in *dressed up like a dog's dinner*—is hardly flattering, we must wonder whether the dog's life really is a happy one.

Dogs

Certain breeds take their names from their countries of origin, or of association, as in the *labrador*, a breed of retriever originally developed in Labrador, a large *peninsula* (from Latin *paene* 'almost' and *insula* 'island') in eastern Canada. Other dogs whose names derive fairly straightforwardly from their places of origin are the *Great Dane* (from Denmark), the *Spaniel* (from Old French *espaignol* 'Spanish'), and the *dalmatian* (from Dalmatia, an area of former Yugoslavia, now part of Croatia and Montenegro). *Alsatian* is another eponym, used for the dog also known as the *German shepherd*—a name that is modelled on the German name for the species: *deutscher Schäferhund. Alsatian* is the adjectival form of *Alsatia,* the name for an area bordering Germany and Switzerland, which is now Alsace, part of France. The *Rottweiler,* or properly *rottweiler Hund*, is so called because it is from Rottweil, a town in Baden-Württemberg in Germany. *Dobermann*, or *Dobermann Pinscher*, is also an eponym, though in this case it is named after a German dog-breeder called Ludwig Dobermann. The origins of *Pinscher* are less clear—it may derive from an area of north-western Austria called *Pinzgau*. An alternative theory is that it is related to the verb *pinch*—perhaps a reference to the dog's docked tail—but this is hard to square with the word's German origins.

Names based on appearance are less common: *greyhound* may seem to be an obvious example, but this actually derives from Old English *grig*, meaning 'bitch'—the switch to *grey* is based on a folk-etymological association with the better-known colour term, and the fact that some greyhounds are indeed grey. But while greyhounds have nothing to do with the colour grey, grizzly bears, which are brown, do. The word *grizzly* is from the French word *gris* 'grey', and refers to the white tips on the ends of their fur. You may have thought that they were called grizzly bears because of their ferocious appearance and nature, but *grizzly* is unrelated to *grisly*—which is from Old English *grislic* 'terrifying'. Even so, they are not recommended as family pets. A dog that probably was named for its colour is *collie*, an alternative form of *coaly*—an adjective used to mean 'covered in coal-dust' or 'black as coal'. The corgi's diminutive size is captured in its name, which is the Welsh for 'dwarf dog', from Welsh *cor* 'dwarf' and *ci* 'dog'. While corgis are undoubtedly small, it is harder to see the connection between the *shih-tzu* and a lion (the name derives from Chinese *shizi* 'lion'). The similarity becomes a little clearer if, instead of picturing a lion prowling the grasslands of Africa, we think of the stylized representations found in oriental art.

Other breeds formerly served their human masters as hunting dogs; their particular skills are reflected in the names they have been given. The *terrier* was trained to flush out vermin, especially badgers, rabbits, and foxes, from their underground burrows. The name derives from the Latin *terrarius* 'earthly', a reference to their ability to dig underground. The animal's relentless persistence (or *doggedness*) in pursuit of its prey has led to the metaphorical use of *terrier* to refer to someone who is similarly tenacious or persistent. The *Jack Russell terrier* takes its name from a renowned breeder, a nineteenth-century clergyman whose fame led to the nickname 'The Sporting Parson'. The *retriever* is also called after its use in flushing out game, rather than its ability to retrieve a stick thrown by its owner. Also named for its use as a hunting dog—specifically its role in digging out badgers—is the *dachshund*, from German *dachs* 'badger'. Another hunting dog whose name is of German extraction is the *poodle*, originally *Pudelhund*, from the verb *puddeln* 'to splash about'. This dog gets its name from its role as a water dog—one trained to retrieve waterfowl when hunting. The *pointer* is called after the distinctive pose it adopts when it detects quarry—pointing its nose and mouth towards the location of the hunted animal, standing stock still, and sometimes lifting one of its legs. Hunting with dogs is also the root of *harass*, now used of unwelcome sexual advances, since it is from the Old French verb *harer*, meaning 'to set a dog upon'.

If your family pet is a horse, you may wish to engage in some *equestrianism*, from the Latin *equus* 'horse'. A less impressive equine specimen was known to the Romans as a *caballus*—the term for a working horse, similar to the English *nag* or *jade* (a worn-out old horse, from which we get *jaded*)—which is the origin of French *cheval* and Spanish *caballo*. The Greek word for a horse was *hippos*, which survives in the personal names *Philip* and *Philippa* (meaning 'horse lover'), and in *hippopotamus* 'river-horse'.

A donkey was originally an *ass*; the word *donkey* was introduced as a colloquial name for this animal in the eighteenth century. The fact that it originally rhymed with *monkey* may indicate that it derives from the colour term *dun*; another suggestion is that it is from the personal name Duncan. The *ass* lies behind the word *easel*, a loanword from the Dutch version *ezel*. Because donkeys were used to carry heavy loads, this frame used for supporting paintings was named after the animal. A similar development is found in our use of the term *clothes horse* to refer to a wooden frame employed as a support for drying clothes.

Depending on the type of horse and your experience, there are various speeds at which you might choose to ride. Slightly faster than walking pace is the *trot*, from which we get *on the trot* 'in succession' and *trot out*, meaning produce a well-rehearsed piece of information. Speedier than the *trot* is the *canter*, which is named after the speed at which medieval pilgrims, like the collection of 'sondry folk' described by Chaucer, would ride on their journey to Canterbury—the location of the shrine of St Thomas à Becket. If you are feeling really confident you might risk a *gallop*; this word is a French borrowing which was adopted in the sixteenth century, when it replaced the variant form *wallop* used in the Middle Ages in works like Thomas Malory's *Le Morte d'Arthur*: 'He rode a grete walop tylle he com to the fountain.'

Since horse-riding was a popular pastime during the British rule in India, a number of the relevant terms are of Indian extraction. The *jodhpurs* worn on the legs when riding are called after the city of that name in western India, where they are worn as part of daily attire. The *gymkhana*, an equestrian meeting that involves jumping fences, egg-and-spoon races on horseback, and other events for children, is based on the Urdu word *gendkanah*, meaning 'racket court', altered by association with the etymologically unrelated *gymnastics*. More ambitious than the gymkhana is the *steeplechase*, a cross-country course with ditches and hedges, which gets its name from the use of a distant steeple to mark the end of the race. Riding for pleasure is also known as *hacking*, from the use of *hack* to refer to an everyday horse for general-purpose riding. This word is a shortening of *Hackney*, a borough of East London, where pasture was provided for horses. It is also the source of *Hackney carriage*—originally a cart drawn by a horse, but now a general word for a taxi.

Instead of actually doing the riding, you may prefer to attend a race meeting and perhaps even have a flutter. If you're feeling lucky, you might choose to *back* an *outsider* or a *long shot*; a more cautious approach would be to have an *each-way bet*—betting on your horse to *place* (finish in the top three or four) or *make the frame* (the wooden frame at racing events on which the top four names appear); alternatively, you could *hedge your bets* by placing a second bet to cover the first—this term derives from the function of a hedge as a form of defence or protection. For an informed decision, you should study the *form sheet*, which records past performances, and hope that the horse runs *true to form*; this is also the origin of the phrase *have form*, used of someone with a record of criminal convictions. But it's not just the horse's form that needs to be taken into consideration, there's also the issue of the particular racecourse; the idea that horses are better suited to some venues than others is enshrined in the saying *horses for courses*. The best way to find out how a particular horse will perform is to ask the animal itself, or get the information *straight from the horse's mouth*. But be careful not to be accused of *looking a gift horse in the mouth*, a proverb which refers to the practice of trying to determine a horse's age by inspecting its teeth (from which we get the expression *long in the tooth*). The idea behind this phrase is that one should gratefully accept a gift without attempting to assess its value.

Horse-Racing

A horse that is expected to win is known as a *banker* or *dead cert* (short for *dead certain*); a *shoo-in* may sound like a *safe bet*, but this term was originally used of a horse winning a race that had been rigged. Since the horse won by such a clear margin, it appeared as if the other racers were shooing it over the finish line. To be avoided are the *also ran*, that fails to place, and the *bismarck*—a favourite that is expected to flop.

Whichever you choose, you'll be hoping that your horse *goes the distance* and *stays the course*, and doesn't end up a *non-starter*—a horse that fails to run at all. Although *pole position* is now more commonly associated with motor-racing, where it refers to the front position on the starting grid, this term originated in horse-racing, referring to the pole used to indicate the most favourable starting location next to the inner rail. If your horse is comfortably ahead as it comes down the *final straight* (US *final stretch*), it may be that the horse will win *hands down*—a reference to the way a jockey drops his hands to relax the reins when victory seems assured. A runner whose lead is so great that the horse can walk to the finish is said to have earned a *walkover*, a term now used of any one-sided contest or easily achievable goal.

If things are close and the race is *going to the wire* (a reference to an imaginary wire marking the finish line), prepare yourself for a *dead heat* (a heat, or race, in which two or more horses reach the *winning post* at the same time) or a *blanket finish*—when the horses finish so close together you could throw a blanket over them. If your horse wins *by a nose* or finishes *in the money*, you can return to the *bookmaker* (or *bookie*) in triumph. This term derives from the practice of recording bets in a notebook (hence *to open* or *keep a book*). If, however, the race is unexpectedly won by a horse that no one has backed, this is a *turn-up* (originally referring to the turning up of a particular card in a game of chance, and hence an unexpected or surprise occurrence) for the bookmakers, or a *turn-up for the books*—a phrase now used to refer to any unexpected slice of good fortune.

Another popular pursuit for animal lovers is a visit to the local bird reserve to huddle up in a hide with fellow *birdwatchers, birders,* and *twitchers.* The latter group are birdwatchers whose main objective is to collect sightings of rare birds; one theory is that the name derives from a tendency to get twitchy when the wind gets up, thereby increasing the likelihood of birds being blown off course. Twitchers are also known as *tickers*, from the practice of ticking off such sightings on a list. Those only interested in making rare sightings are rather looked down upon by serious *ornithologists*—the term for scientists who engage in the study of birds. This word derives from the Greek *ornis* 'bird', cognate with the Old English word *earn* 'eagle'. The Latin word for bird, *avis*, is the root of *avian* 'pertaining to birds', *aviary* 'large enclosure for birds', as well as *aviation*, the term for the science of powered flight. The word *bird* is of Old English origin, although it referred more specifically to a little bird. The general term for a bird in Old English was *fugol*, the ancestor of modern English *fowl*, now used of domestic cocks and hens.

In addition to being an enjoyable pursuit, birdwatching can be useful for fortune-telling—as is apparent from the etymology of *auspicious* 'conducive to success, favourable'. This word has its origins in Latin *auspex* (from *avis* and *specere* 'to observe'), the name given by the Romans to a person who predicted the future by observing the flight of birds. Something that is auspicious is thus an event that has been given the auspex's blessing—the root of the phrase *under the auspices of*. A similar origin lies behind the phrase *augurs well*, which originally referred to a positive prediction by an *augur*—an alternative term for the *auspex*; this word is the source of *inaugurate*, referring to a consecration or installation carried out having taken omens from the flight of birds.

Birds

Many of the names of common birds are self-evident: try identifying a *blackbird* to a child and observe the withering look of scorn you receive. This name replaced the older *ouzel*, first recorded in Old English and later spelled *woosell*, as in Shakespeare's reference to the 'Woosell cock, so blacke of hewe / With Orange tawny bill' in *A Midsummer Night's Dream*. This word may be connected to the Latin word for the same bird—*merula*—the source of another name for the bird, *merle*, used mostly in Scots dialect poetry. John Florio's English–Italian dictionary of 1598, *A Worlde of Wordes*, adds a further name in the *black-mack* found in his entry for *Merula*: 'a birde called a black-mack, and owzell, a mearle, a black bird'.

The name of the robin may appear less obvious until we recall that it was earlier known as the *redbreast*. It was only later that the bird acquired the first name—initially Robert, and later Robin. The earliest recorded English name for the bird is the *ruddock*—still used in some dialects—which is derived from the colour term *red*. In the case of other birds the connection between name and markings is no longer so apparent. But once you know that the Old English word *steort* meant 'tail', you will immediately understand where the *redstart* got its name. Similarly, the *redpoll* takes its name from a Germanic word *poll* 'head', which still survives in the name of the *poll tax*. The *wheatear* sounds as if it's connected to ears of wheat but in fact this is a corruption—or a cleaning-up—of an earlier form *whiteeres, or white-arse*, a reference to the colour of the bird's rump. The origins of the *bunting* are unclear, although some scholars have suggested a link with the Scots word *buntin* 'plump', or with the Welsh *bontinog* 'large-buttocked'—neither of which is especially flattering. The second element of *magpie* is from the Latin name for the bird: *pica*. The first element of the name is a later addition taken from the girl's name *Margery*, reflecting a tendency for birds to acquire personal names. Other examples are the *jackdaw* (formerly the *daw*), *house martin, jenny wren*, and, of course, the *robin*.

Additional sources of birds' names are features of behaviour—flight, song, and feeding habits. If you've ever observed the speedy, darting flight of the *swift*, you will have no difficulty imagining how it acquired that name. The well-known tree-drilling habits of the *woodpecker* are also plainly the source of its name. The *chaffinch* is christened after its habit of searching out grain from the *chaff*, or husks of grain, found in barns. The name of the *linnet* is borrowed from Old French *linette*, itself from the word *lin*, referring to the flax plant from which the bird gets its food. The *brambling* gets its name from its close association with bramble bushes; the *nuthatch* is probably related to the verb *hack*, referring to the bird's practice of clamping nuts within the bark of the tree so as to hack at them with its beak.

The *nightingale* is most famous for its song; knowing that the Old English verb *galan* meant 'to sing' helps explain why the nocturnal *nightingale* is so called. Also christened for their singing are the *serins*, whose name goes back to the classical word *siren*, the name of the mermaids that lured sailors to their doom with their song, best known from Homer's *Odyssey*. Other names represent attempts to reflect the song itself, using *onomatopoeia* (from a Greek word meaning 'word-making'). In the case of the *cuckoo* and *hoopoe* this connection is still apparent, since the names remain accurate approximations of the birds' calls. In other instances the pronunciation and reference of the name have diverged considerably; *pigeon*, for instance, is from Latin *pipio*, coined by the Romans to describe the cheeping sound of a young bird—a long way from the cooing sound associated with the pigeon. The word *rook* is an attempt to render the bird's harsh call; it goes back to the same root as the Greek verb meaning 'to croak'. The chattering sound of birds of the *chat* family gives them their name; in the case of the *stonechat*, its call was thought to resemble the sound of two stones being knocked together.

If you are more interested in birds of prey than songbirds, you might try your hand at hawking—ensuring you are wearing a substantial glove, of course. Hawking comes with a variety of abstruse terminology; mastery of the complex lexicon associated with the noble pursuits of hawking and hunting was a badge of social status in the Middle Ages. According to medieval legend, these terms were first introduced by Sir Tristram, one of the knights of King Arthur's celebrated round table; in his fifteenth-century Arthurian epic, *Le Morte d'Arthur*, Thomas Malory praised such 'goodly tearmys' whereby 'men of worshyp may discover a jentylman frome a yoman and a yoman frome a vylayne'. So if you're thinking of giving hawking a go, or just want to avoid being mistaken for a villain (in its earlier sense of 'peasant'), be sure to learn the following goodly terms.

Hawking

If you're serious about taking up this hobby, you can get a good sense of the practicalities involved in training a bird for hunting from Helen Macdonald's moving memoir *H is for Hawk*, where she recounts her attempts to train a goshawk, a bird which takes its name from the Old English *gos* 'goose' and *hafoc* 'hawk'. The Old French name for the bird, *austruchier*, gives us the modern English term for a keeper of goshawks: *austringer*. The goshawk should not be confused with the similar-looking peregrine falcon, whose name is taken from the Latin *peregrinus* 'foreign' or 'pilgrim' (*per* 'through' and *ager* 'field'), so called because they were trapped by falconers when on migration (a kind of pilgrimage), rather than being taken from the nest. An adult bird caught in the wild is known as a *haggard*; such birds were considered more difficult to tame and more likely to go astray: this is the sense invoked in Othello's reference to Desdemona being proved a haggard in Shakespeare's play. In modern English this word describes someone worn out and exhausted by anxiety. A juvenile bird caught while on migration is known as a *passage hawk* or *passager*, while a bird taken from the nest is termed an *eyas*. Deriving ultimately from Latin *nidus* 'nest', the spelling of this word is the result of a false division, by which *a neyas* was mistakenly understood to be *an eyas*; a similar process lies behind words like *adder, apron*, and *umpire* (compare earlier *nadder, napron*, and *noumpere* 'no peer'). A hawk whose talons have been removed is called a *poltroon*, a word which survives today in the sense 'worthless wretch' or 'coward'.

If you want to fit in with your fellow falconers, you need to be careful how you employ the term *falcon*, since amongst the initiated it is only used of the female bird. This word derives from Latin *falco*, from a word for 'sickle', inspired by the similarity of this blade to the bird's hooked talons. The male bird is known as the *tercel*, from Latin *tertius* 'third'. This name may be a reference to its diminutive size, since the male is approximately a third smaller than the female. An alternative theory, however, links the name to the belief that the third egg in a clutch would produce a male bird. Goshawks belong to the genus known by the Latin term *accipiter*, from a root meaning 'swift feather'. These short-winged hawks are also termed *ignoble* birds for their tendency to chase after (or *rake*) their quarry in a rather inelegant manner. By contrast, long-winged hawks, which seize their quarry in a single graceful swoop, are considered *noble* birds.

But sounding like a competent falconer is more than simply knowing the correct names for the birds. You'll also need to master the proper way to refer to its various parts and behaviour. Reference to the bird's *wings, claws*, or *tail* will immediately expose you as a novice; to an experienced falconer these are *sails, pounces*, and *train*. Confusingly, the part of the bird's leg between thigh and foot is known as an *arm*. There are no fewer than three terms to describe the way the bird wipes its beak after feeding: *feaking, sewing*, or *sniting*. When the bird beats its wings impatiently in an attempt to fly off the perch, it is *bating* (from the French *battre* 'beat'). The sport's gentlemanly origins are evident from its genteel euphemisms: hawks don't defecate, they *mute*, while vomiting is *casting* or *gleaming*—perhaps the result of *gurgiting* 'choking after having taken too large a mouthful'—a problem not limited to hawks. Hearty drinking by a hawk is known as *bousing*—again, a characteristic it shares with some of its human handlers. A hawk that is in the proper condition to hunt is *in yarak*, from a Persian word meaning 'power' or 'strength'.

The tools of the falconer's trade include *jesses*, leather straps that fit through the anklets and the *cadge* (related to *cage*: a wooden frame on which the hawk is carried to the field); even the leather ring used to attach a bell to the bird's leg—enabling it to be tracked when in flight—has its own term: *bewet*. The *creance*, a long line which prevents the half-trained hawk from flying away, takes its name from Old French *créance* 'trust, confidence' (also the source of modern English *credence*), since it was used to restrain a bird that could not yet be fully trusted to return to the handler.

PART V

Evening

CHAPTER 16

Going out

———— ☾ ————

Perhaps you like to spend your evenings expanding your cultural horizons. If so, you may wish to head to an art gallery or museum. A *gallery* was originally a long narrow room or covered walkway, from the Italian *galleria*; in medieval Latin it referred to a church porch. Its ultimate etymology remains unclear, although it may be an alteration of Galilee, the name given to the northern region of Palestine. The church porch was likened to the region of Galilee in being an outlying section of the church where outsiders were located and furthest from the *altar* (the table on which the consecrated bread and wine are placed, from Latin *altus* 'high'); the choir, where the stalls occupied by the monks were positioned, was considered to be like Jerusalem—the centre of the Holy Land.

While a gallery is etymologically connected to part of Palestine, the original museum was founded in 280 BC by Ptolemy I of Egypt. The word *museum* is Greek in origin; it is from *mouseion* 'seat of the muses'—the daughters of Zeus and Mnemosyne, the goddess of memory—also related to *mnemonic*, an aid to memory. The nine muses presided over the arts and sciences, with each muse representing a different branch of enquiry; Erato, whose name means 'lovely', was the muse of lyric poetry, Clio, from Greek *kleiein* 'to celebrate', was the Muse of history, while Urania, meaning 'heavenly one', was responsible for astronomy. The name *muse* goes back to a Greek root meaning 'song'—it is the source of the English word *music*. It is, however, unrelated to the English verb *muse* 'be absorbed in thought, ponder', which derives from an Old French verb meaning 'meditate, reflect'. The French verb *muser* is probably from a noun meaning 'face', also the root of *muzzle*—originally the term for an animal's mouth or snout, and now a guard to prevent it from biting.

Alternatively, you may prefer to get your fix of culture by attending a dramatic performance at the theatre. The theatre takes its name from its principal function; the word originates in the Greek verb *theasthai* 'to look at'. The audience, however, are defined by their role as hearers rather than watchers, since the word is from *audire* 'to hear'—the root of *auditorium, audition*, as well as *audit*—originally a legal process at which accounts were read aloud. An *amphitheatre*, from Greek *amphi* 'on both sides', was a classical theatre in which a central stage was surrounded by a circle of tiered seating from which the action could be observed on all sides.

The Stage

The Greeks used the term *comedy* to refer to a comic drama or literary work—its origins lie in the word *komos* 'revel'. *Tragedy* is also Greek in origin; it originally described a tragic play or solemn poem. The word appears to derive from *tragos* 'he-goat'; the connection may have originated in the offering of a male goat as a prize in a writing contest. *Melodrama* is from Greek *melos* 'song' (also the source of *melody*) and *drama* 'deed, act'. Today, melodramatic has acquired negative connotations of overly emotional; a similar development can be traced in the word *histrionics*, which originally meant 'theatrical' (from Latin *histrio* 'actor') but now implies 'excessively dramatic'—often used of the attention-seeking behaviour of small children or professional footballers. The Latin term for a stage play was *ludicrum*, from *ludo* 'I play', which gives us the adjective *ludicrous*—originally meaning 'pertaining to a game' or 'intended in play', this word has also taken on pejorative overtones.

The establishment of Greek tragedy is credited to the poet Thespis, from whose name we have derived the word *thespian* to refer to an actor. The Greek term for an actor, or anyone prone to pretence and dissembling, was *hupokrites*—from which we get the English word *hypocrite*. *Actor*, from Latin *agere* 'to do', initially a legal term referring to a plaintiff, came to be used of a stage performer in the sixteenth century. A *ham actor*, one who through over-enthusiasm has a tendency to exaggerate unconvincingly, is nothing to do with cold meat; it probably originates in a variant form of *amateur*— etymologically someone who performs for love (Latin *amare* 'to love') rather than money. The Greek term *pantomimos*, meaning 'imitator of all', originally denoted a mime artist who acted out mythological tales using gestures and actions, and subsequently a comedy based on stock characters. It is the origin of the term *pantomime*, used of the traditional British Christmas entertainment in which B-list celebrities perform folk tales like Dick Whittington, Jack and the Beanstalk, and Aladdin. Such performances typically involve repeated *innuendoes* (from a Latin word meaning 'nodding at, intimating'), cross-dressing, and plenty of *slapstick*—originally a device comprising two flat pieces of wood that was used to generate the sound of someone being slapped, used to accompany a feigned blow in popular comedy performances.

A number of idioms are theatrical in origin. Perhaps most evident is the phrase *behind the scenes*, now used to refer to something not subject to public access, but originally the area behind the stage where the audience is not permitted to enter—the word *scene* is from Greek *scena*, which could refer to the stage itself as well as the scenery. *Waiting in the wings* has a fairly obvious theatrical origin, since it refers to the side of the stage where an actor waits to make an appearance on stage. Perhaps less clearly connected is *wing it*, meaning 'speak or act without preparation', which originated in the way an actor playing a part at short notice would be helped by the presence of a prompter hidden in the wings. *Stealing the limelight*, referring to the light used to draw attention to the leading actors, is now used of any attempt to direct more attention to oneself. When the theatre director John Dennis (1657–1734) heard that a rival company had adopted his mode of simulating thunder for a production of *Macbeth*, he is recorded to have accused the company of having *stolen his thunder*. Another theatrical term reflecting our inclination to divert attention from another to ourselves is to *upstage* someone. *Upstage* is the term for the back of the stage; by positioning themselves upstage of another member of the cast, actors are able to compel that person to turn towards them and thus away from the audience.

The break during a play for drinks and ice creams is known as an *interval*; this can be used of any break in an activity, but it originates in Latin *intervallum*, referring to the space between ramparts. During the lengthy medieval mystery plays, which frequently lasted all day, it was usual to break up the seriousness with a light drama known as an *interlude*, literally meaning 'between play'. The *role* played by an actor in a drama comes from Latin *rotulus* 'little wheel', and refers to the roll of paper on which an actor's part was written.

At the end of a performance it is usual for the audience to *applaud* (from Latin *plaudere* 'to clap'); while most modern audiences clap spontaneously, Roman actors had to demand their round of applause using the imperative form *plaudite* 'applaud!' From this we get the word *plaudit*, meaning 'expression of praise or approval'. Less obviously related is *plausible*—the connection being that something considered plausible (that is, 'reasonable' or 'likely') was also deemed to be potentially worthy of applause. If a performance falls below expectation, the audience may be more likely to heckle than applaud. *Heckle* was originally a term describing the preparation of flax by splitting and combing the fibres before spinning. The modern meaning, referring to the interruption and haranguing of a public speaker, developed from a Scots usage describing the process of cross-questioning a witness in order to test the validity of a statement. A similar metaphorical development can be seen in *tease*; now used in the sense 'make fun of someone', *tease* also originated as a term for the process of separating the fibres of wool or flax in preparation for spinning. In Rome a poor actor ran the risk of being *exploded*, since *explodere* meant 'to hiss off the stage' or 'to drive out by clapping'—despite the spelling, it too is based upon *plaudere*.

The word *orchestra* originated in the Greek word *orkheisthai* 'to dance'; its earliest use was to refer to the semi-circular area in front of a stage where the chorus danced and sang in Greek theatre. From this it came to be used of the area set down below the front of the stage where the orchestra is situated during a theatrical performance, and from this to refer to the group of instrumentalists located there. For an alternative cultural experience you could attend a concert, or even dust off the instrument you learned at school and give your own performance.

Musical Instruments

The names given to several instruments are straightforwardly descriptive of their shape, or of the sound they make. The small flute known as the *piccolo* is from the Italian word meaning 'small', while the *bassoon* is from Latin *bassus* 'low'. A *piano* was originally a *pianoforte*—still used in some traditional contexts. This name is a contraction of the Italian *piano e forte*, meaning 'soft and loud'—a reference to the way the instrument allows the player to produce a gradation in tone, thereby distinguishing it from the harpsichord. *Piano* and *forte* are the origins of the abbreviations *p* and *f* used to mark dynamics on a musical score, along with the variants *pp* (*pianissimo* 'very soft'), *mp* (*mezzo-piano* 'half-soft'), and *più piano* 'softer' (from Latin *plus* 'more'). Also of Italian extraction are the terms *diminuendo* 'getting softer' (from an Italian word meaning 'diminishing') and *crescendo* 'getting louder' (from an Italian word meaning 'increasing'). The latter is often used today more loosely to refer to a climax, or peak of intensity, especially in the phrase *reach a crescendo*—much to the vexation of etymological pedants. For those who would see this as a recent corruption or misuse, it is worth noting that it has a longer and more distinguished history than one might assume—it is first recorded in F. Scott Fitzgerald's novel *The Great Gatsby* (1925).

Other instruments are named after the manner in which they are played. *Percussion* is from the Latin verb *percutere* 'to strike, beat', referring to the way percussion instruments are played by striking, or hitting two instruments together. Instruments sounded in this way include the aptly named *Glockenspiel*, a German word meaning 'bell play', the *drum*, whose name may imitate its sound, and the *cymbal*, whose name—from Greek *kumbe* 'cup'—references its shape. The *xylophone* is named after the material out of which it is constructed, since *xylo* is a Greek element meaning 'of wood'—a component found in several other technical terms known only to scientists and Scrabble players.

Another instrument whose name contains a reference to the wood out of which it is made is the *oboe*, derived from the French *haut-bois* 'high wood'. A similar instrument, whose name is also of French origin, is the *cor anglais*, which means 'English horn'. While an English horn having a French name may seem odd, the reverse is true of the *French horn*. The *trumpet* is a diminutive form of *trump*—an earlier name for the trumpet or a blast on the horn (from which the slang sense 'break wind' arose). Another instrument whose name is a variant of *trump* is the *trombone*, from Old French *trompe* 'trumpet', while *tuba* takes its name directly from the war-trumpet used by the Romans. The small version of a trumpet known as the *cornet* draws upon Latin *cornu* 'horn', reflecting the origins of the instrument in an animal's horn. The similarity in shape explains the spread of this word to other objects, such as the cone-shaped wafer filled with ice cream. The *clarinet* is a diminutive form of French *clarine*, the name given to a type of bell, from Latin *clarus* 'clear'. It is related to a *clarion call*, now a call to action, but originally the sound made by a trumpet with which an army was summoned to battle.

The closely related instruments known as the *viol, viola*, and *violin*, and even the *cello* (a clipped form of *violoncello*), are all linked to medieval Latin *vidula*, which may derive from an association with the Roman goddess of joy, known as *Vitula*. The word may also be the source of the Germanic word for the same instrument, *fiddle*, now also used to refer to a swindle or confidence trick. Someone taking a leading role in an enterprise is said to *play first fiddle*, while a more subordinate role is described as *playing second fiddle*. When the time comes to renounce a role, one must *hang up one's fiddle*. People in good shape have been *as fit as a fiddle* since the seventeenth century. To *have one's face made of a fiddle* is an obsolete phrase used to describe someone who is particularly attractive; by contrast, someone whose face is *as long as a fiddle* is considered to look especially miserable. *Guitar* is a borrowing of the Spanish word *guitarra*, which is derived from the Greek *kithara*, the name for an instrument resembling the lyre. Unrelated to all of these is the *ukulele*, whose name is from a Hawaiian word meaning 'jumping flea'—the nickname of a particularly energetic exponent.

The musical term *chord*, referring to a group of notes sounded at the same time, derives from *accord*, in the sense 'bring into harmony'. It first appeared in English in the fifteenth century, when it was spelled *corde*; this spelling survives in *accordion*. The word we now spell *cord* is a borrowing of the French word *corde* 'string, rope', which is derived from the Latin *chorda*. It is first recorded in

English in the fifteenth century as *cord*; however, in the sixteenth century it was re-spelled as *chord* to reflect its Latin origins. This spelling remained common in the seventeenth and eighteenth centuries; it has survived into modern usage in certain specialized senses, such as *touched a chord*, and in the name of the *harpsichord*. In the eighteenth century, the musical cord was confused with this word and this triggered a change of spelling to *chord*; in the meantime the word *chord* lost its 'h' and reverted to *cord*. So, while the spelling of these two words might appear straightforward, their histories show that the spellings are, etymologically speaking, the wrong way round. *Chord* should refer to the rope, and the musical term should be *cord*. If you don't play an instrument, perhaps you could try singing *a cappella*. This term, referring to singing performed without instrumental accompaniment, literally means 'in the style of the chapel', referring back to the monastic chanting and plainsong of the Christian liturgy.

If the carnival happens to be in town, you might decide to pay a visit. The word *carnival* is based upon Latin *caro* 'meat' (as in *carnivore*); the association derives from an early use of *carnival* to refer to the indulgence that preceded the period of fasting known as Lent. During Lent, Christians were expected to forgo such indulgences and to put away, or *levare*, the meat—from which we get the word *carnival*. *Lent* (earlier *Lenten*) takes its name from *long*—since the period of Lent coincides with the lengthening of the days in spring. If you have a taste for trapeze artists, fire-eaters, and lion tamers, you might prefer to visit the *circus*. Its name derives from the Roman *circus* (also the word for a circle)—the venue for chariot racing and *gladiator* (from Latin *gladius* 'sword') fights.

Another option for your evening's entertainment is a trip to the cinema. *Cinema* is an abbreviated form of *cinematograph*, from Greek *kinema* 'movement' (compare the modern alternative, *movies*); it was borrowed into English from French, hence the soft 's' pronunciation of the 'c'. An alternative pronunciation with a hard 'k', reflecting the Greek etymology, was initially adopted by some—reflected in the rare alternative spelling *kinema*. Going to the cinema today will often mean visiting an *Odeon*; the proprietary name of this cinema chain is from Greek *odeion*, referring to a building employed for musical performance—originally the name of an edifice constructed by Pericles in Athens. The word *Odeon* is related to *ode*, a lyric poem—originally one that was intended to be sung—which is from the Greek word for a song.

CHAPTER 17

Drinking

—————— ☾ ——————

As soon as the performance has concluded, it's time to head out for a drink or two at a local bar, hostelry, or *pub* (an abbreviation of *public house*). Terms for those who frequent drinking dens were often evocatively descriptive, such as *swill-bowl, spigot-sucker, rinse-pitcher,* and *gulch-cup*—all of which describe the process of emptying a drinking vessel. The word *toss-pot*, now a general term of abuse, was initially a name for a drunkard, referring to the tendency to *toss off*, that is, tilt back and thereby empty, the pot containing drink. Terms drawing on classical roots sound less disreputable; these include *potator*, the Latin term for a drinker (from *potare* 'to drink'), *polyposist*, from a Greek word meaning 'hard drinker', and *son of Bacchus*—the Roman name for the god of wine known to the Greeks as Dionysus. Less convivial company is the *shot-clog*—a sixteenth-century term for an unwelcome drinking companion who is tolerated simply because he pays the bill at the end of the evening. In the eighteenth century, someone who was frequently drunk was known as a *lush*; in the nineteenth century they could be termed a *Lushington*. This is from a society of that name that convened at the Harp Tavern on Russell Street, with an appointed Lord Mayor and four aldermen, who controlled the wards known as Juniper, Poverty, Lunacy, and Suicide.

Now in the company of your fellow-drinkers, or *ale-knights*, it is time to sample a favourite *beverage* (going back to Latin *bibere* 'to drink'), or tipple. *Tipple* was originally *tippler*, someone who sold rather than drank alcohol, perhaps from a regional Norwegian word *tipla* 'to drip slowly'. *Booze* is one of a small number of words borrowed into English from Dutch in the Middle Ages; it comes from a word meaning 'to drink deeply', related to *buise*, the name of a large drinking cup. *Beer* and *ale* are both derived from Old English, while *lager* is from German *Lagerbier*, a term that describes beer that has been brewed to be kept, from the German word *Lager* 'storehouse'. The dark bitter known as *porter* is so called because it was originally made for porters, whose duties involved carrying—hence their name, from Latin *portare* 'to carry'. This is the source of the French verb *porter*, which can also mean 'to wear'—hence *prêt-à-porter* 'ready to wear', used of clothes bought off the peg as opposed to made to measure. The Latin word for a cask, or a wineskin, *buttis*, lies behind the English word *bottle*; it also survives in the word *butt*, the term still used for a cask in which wine or beer is stored, and in *butler*. The French word for a butler, *sommelier*, is now used in posh restaurants for the waiter in charge of wine orders.

Before drinking it is traditional to *raise a glass*, or *drink a toast*—naming someone in whose honour, or to whose health, the drink is dedicated. The formula 'Here's to X' can be traced back to the seventeenth century—it is first recorded in *Romeo and Juliet*—although since the glass Romeo raises to Juliet contains poison, it's not the most auspicious beginning to the tradition. If you can't think of anyone to dedicate the drink to, or if there's no one suitable among the assembled drinkers, the safest bet is to plump for absent friends. Although the similarity may not be obvious, the toast you drink is related to the toast you eat: the connection being that the former originated in the idea that raising a glass to a particular lady flavoured the contents in a similar way as the spiced toast that was added to drinks in the eighteenth century. As an alternative, you could fall back on *Cheers*: the plural of *cheer*, expressing a wish for cheerfulness and good spirits. In the Middle Ages the appropriate toast was *Wassail*, a salutation borrowed from the Danish Vikings who settled in Britain. The word derives from the Old Norse *ves heill*—the equivalent of the Old English *wes hal* 'be in good health'.

The correct response—should you ever find yourself drinking with a Viking—is *Drinkhail* 'drink good health'. The word *wassail* was also used to refer to the spiced ale drunk at Twelfth Night and Christmas, and then to all kinds of general revelry—as in Hamlet's reference to the king's keeping wassail and draining his draughts of Rhenish—a wine produced in the region surrounding the Rhine.

Another toast borrowed from the Scandinavian languages is *skol*, adopted in Scotland in the seventeenth century, and derived from the Old Norse *skal* 'bowl'. In the nineteenth century the Gaelic *Sláinte*, meaning 'health', became popular in Scotland and Ireland. The French word for health, *santé*, also used as a drinking toast, has been recorded in English since the beginning of the twentieth century. From German, English also borrowed the exclamation *Prosit* (or *prost*); despite its Germanic extraction, this word has its origins in a Latin word meaning 'may it benefit'. From Anglo-Chinese we get the toast *Chin chin*, originating in Chinese *ts'ing ts'ing*. More exotic variants coined in the 1920s include *Here's to the skin off your nose* and *Here's mud in your eye*, used by the likes of Bertie Wooster and even Jeeves, albeit with an appropriate unease as to the decorum: 'Skin off your nose, Jeeves.' 'Mud in your eye, sir, if I may use the expression.'

Drink

Alcohol is from the Arabic *al-kuhl*, the name given to a powder used as a cosmetic, especially for darkening the eyes. In later applications it referred to an essence formed by the process of distillation, from which its modern use derived. *Wine* is an early loanword from Latin *vinum*, probably borrowed by the Angles and Saxons when they came into contact with Roman soldiers, even before the invasion of Britain. The Greek word for wine, *oinos*, gives us *oenomania*, which can mean both 'a passion for wine' and a 'craving for alcohol'—a helpful ambiguity that suggests either a wine buff or a drunkard. *Dipsomania* may be more euphemistic in its original Greek etymology—it literally means 'thirst madness'—but its English use is considerably blunter, being defined simply as 'alcoholism'.

Champagne is titled after the wine-producing region in eastern France where it is made, which in turn takes its name from the Latin *campania* 'level country' (from *campus* 'field'). At the other end of the scale of price and sophistication is *plonk*—originally an Australian slang term derived from *vin blanc* 'white wine'. Also originating in a description of its colour is the word *claret*, which is from the Old French *vin claret* 'clear wine'—initially used to refer to a light wine. It was only later that *claret* came to refer to red wines in general, and then specifically those produced in the Bordeaux region. Also named for its appearance is the Spanish drink *sangria*, in which red wine is blended with lemonade and fruit, which translates as 'bleeding'.

Another source of names for alcoholic beverages are their places of origin. Thus *port* is so called because it was imported from the Portuguese port of Oporto. *Sherry* is from Spanish *vino de Xeres*, wine of Xeres (the older name for Jerez)—the 'x' having initially been pronounced 'sh'. This was initially adopted into English as *sherris*; because this word was mistakenly understood to be plural, the singular form *sherry* was born.

When gin was introduced into England in the seventeenth century, it was erroneously believed to have been produced in the city of Geneva—leading to a folk-etymological form *geneva*. But *gin* in fact originates in the Dutch word *genever*, from Latin *juniperus* 'juniper', since juniper berries were used to flavour the spirit. The eighteenth century witnessed the establishment of the *gin shop* and the *gin house*, a public house that specialized in selling gin, and sometimes also produced it. By the nineteenth century these had been joined by the *gin palace*, a larger establishment that was typically gaudily and ostentatiously decorated. Gin and tonic was first introduced to the British through the army in India; the idea behind the concoction was to make it easier for the soldiers to take the quinine in the soda, which was a preventative treatment for malaria.

Often drunk for its supposed medicinal properties, *whisky* is a contraction of *whiskybae*, a rendering in English of the Gaelic *uisgebeatha* 'water of life'. Today *whisky* is the Scots spelling while *whiskey* is Irish, but this is an artificial distinction introduced by the whisk(e)y industry. The word *uisce* is related to the English equivalent *water*; both go back to a root that is also preserved in Latin *unda* 'wave', from which we get *inundated*. Another spirit whose name is connected with the word for water is Russian *vodka*, which is simply the diminutive form of *voda* 'water'.

Spirits mixed with water are known as *grog*—a term that originally referred to rum that had been watered down. The name is taken from *Old Grog*, the nickname of Admiral Vernon, who was the first to instruct that the rum served to sailors be diluted with water. His nickname is taken from his habit of wearing a cloak made from *grogram*, a fabric whose name is drawn from the French *gros grain* 'coarse grain'. Adding too much water to a drink is known as *drowning the miller*, or *putting the miller's eye out*—also used of putting too much water into the dough when baking bread.

If you want to avoid getting drunk, all you need to do is drop an amethyst in your drink. The word *amethyst* comes from Greek *amethustos* 'not drunken', a name which originated in the belief that the connection between the colour of the stone and that of red wine would prevent a drinker from becoming intoxicated. But if you've left your protective amethyst at home, it's possible you are beginning to feel a little *tipsy*—from *tip over*, referring to an inability to walk or stand upright. Or perhaps a more appropriate epithet would be one of the numerous English terms for being drunk. These include cooking terms likening the drunkard to one who has been *pickled*, or *stewed* (*to the ears, eyebrows,* or *gills*) in alcohol, alongside *sloshed, sozzled, tight,* and *half-cut.* More formal, though typically used with mock-seriousness, is *inebriated,* from Latin *ebrius* 'drunk', or the euphemistic *tired and emotional.*

Another way of expressing the level of drunkenness is by means of a simile—English is suitably well stocked with examples. While you may be familiar with *drunk as a lord* or the rhyming *drunk as a skunk,* there are a number of less well-known examples, including *drunk as a mouse, drunk as a rat* (from which we get *ratted* and *rat-arsed*), *drunk as a beggar, drunk as a fiddler,* and *drunk as a wheelbarrow*—the last of these presumably a reference to the difficulty of maintaining a straight line when pushing this three-wheeled cart, especially when heavily laden. *Sturdy* may appear to have little in common with these inebriated animals, but its etymon, the Old French word *esturdi* 'dazed', may be derived ultimately from Latin *turdus* 'thrush', recalling the unsteady manner with which thrushes walk after eating grapes that have been partially fermented. In French a drunkard may be described as *soûl comme une grive*: 'drunk as a thrush'.

If you have really overindulged you may find yourself *whipping the cat, flaying the fox, praying to the porcelain goddess,* or *talking to Ralph on the big white telephone.* These are just some of the more unusual recorded idioms referring to being sick, *vomiting* (from Latin *vomo* 'I am sick'), or—more euphemistically—*losing one's dinner.* The word *vomit* also appears in *vomitorium,* the name of the room to which Romans were reputed to retire after an evening's excessive eating and drinking in order to be sick. But this is a twentieth-century myth; in reality a vomitorium was the passage that led into an amphitheatre by which members of the audience would enter and exit—this use of the word meaning 'pass out' rather than 'be sick'.

All of this heavy drinking may lead to a hangover. The classic hangover cure known as *the hair of the dog*—essentially an invitation to carry on drinking, thereby postponing rather than curing the suffering—is a shortened version of *the hair of the dog that bit you*. This saying arose during the sixteenth century, when it was believed that the best way to treat a dog bite was to apply hair taken from the same animal that inflicted the wound. This was the advice offered to Samuel Pepys after a night's heavy drinking and which, despite reservations, he found to be effective in relieving his pounding head: 'at noon dined with Sir W. Batten and Pen, who would needs have me drink two drafts of sack to-day to cure me of last night's disease, which I thought strange, but I think find it true.' Of course it may be that you are not a big drinker, or perhaps even *teetotal*. This term for someone who abstains entirely from alcohol originates in the temperance movement of the nineteenth century. In order to stress the importance of total abstinence, the first letter was repeated; hence: *T-Total*.

Either way, it is that time of night when you might be tempted to risk a visit to a local nightclub or *discothèque*. Now more common in its abbreviated form *disco*, this word was coined on the model of the French word *bibliothèque* 'library', and was originally used of a record library. An American slang term for a nightclub, from the African-American creole term *juke* 'disorderly', is the origin of the *juke box*. But in a nightclub you don't have any choice over the music; instead you are at the mercy of the *disc jockey*. This may seem like an odd conjunction, since jockeys are associated with riding horses rather than spinning discs. The explanation lies in the history of the word *jockey*, which began life as a variant of the personal name *Jack*—meaning 'lad' or 'bloke'—and was subsequently applied to those whose profession involves riding a horse—couriers and postillions, for example. A later extension saw it refer to labourers engaged in driving and maintaining other forms of transport, such as *garage jockeys, trolley jockeys*, and *motor jockeys*. From this, a further widening led to the birth of the *disc jockey*, or *DJ*.

On the dance floor you may attempt to *jive*, originally a dance performed to jazz music. If you are feeling especially confident, you might decide to attempt a tango; you'll need to identify a willing partner, of course, since *it takes two to tango*—a phrase that emphasizes shared responsibility in a particular situation. The word *tango* looks as if it should be from Latin, since *tango* means 'I touch', preserved in *tangible*, but in fact it is thought to be of African origin. The *flamenco* dance takes its name from the Spanish word for 'Fleming', used here in the sense 'gypsy-like'. It's unclear how this dance acquired an association with gypsies; it may be from uses of the word to mean 'jaunty' and 'attractive'. The usual Spanish term for Gypsy is *gitano*, which originated in a word meaning 'Egyptian'; the same origin lies behind the English word *Gypsy*, or *Gyptian* as it was originally (the form adopted by Philip Pullman in *His Dark Materials*). The reason behind this name is that the Romany people were popularly believed to have originated in Egypt. In fact the Romany, whose language is a form of Hindi, are natives of South Asia. The dance known as the *tarantella* is connected to the *tarantula* (named after the southern Italian town of Taranto) since it was thought to be a cure for *tarantism*—a psychological illness, understood to be caused by a bite from the spider, in which the sufferer experienced an extreme urge to dance.

CHAPTER 18

Staying in

$$\mathbb{C}$$

If engaging in cultural stimulation or heavy drinking sounds too exhausting, you could just stay in and watch the television. The name of this newfangled invention—a compound of Greek *tele* 'far off' and Latin *visio* 'sight'—was derided by the journalist C. P. Scott: 'The word is half Greek, half Latin. No good can come of it.' *Radio* (from Latin *radius* 'ray') is a shortening of *radio-telegraph*—a reference to its use as a means of communication without the need for the connecting wire employed by the electric telegraph, in which messages were tapped out letter by letter using Morse code. We are so accustomed to associating the word *broadcast* with its modern meaning, referring to the way a radio or TV programme is disseminated, we can forget that the word originally described the scattering of seed widely over a surface, rather than in neat rows. The word *disseminated* shows a similar metaphorical extension, since it was originally used to refer to dispersing seeds (from Latin *semen* 'seed'). This metaphor goes back to the origins of radio programming; it was adopted for the name of the British Broadcasting Company (later Corporation) by its first managing director, John Reith, when it was founded in 1922. A radio or TV series comprises individual *episodes*; this word takes us back to Greek drama, where it referred to a section of commentary between songs performed by the chorus in a Greek tragedy.

If there's nothing on the radio or the telly you could choose to watch a film, or binge-watch the latest box set—that is, view numerous episodes in one sitting. *Binge-watching*, a jocular formation based on the pattern of the more serious indulgences *binge-eating* and *binge-drinking*, was introduced in the 1990s, but reached its peak in 2014 when Netflix released the entire second season of *House of Cards* simultaneously. The word *binge* was originally a dialect term from the Midlands meaning 'soak'—the idea of a heavy drinker being someone who absorbs alcohol lies behind terms like *old soak* and *sponge*. The use of *binge* to refer to a heavy-drinking session originated in the slang used by students at Oxford University.

If you fancy an activity that is more cerebrally challenging, you could challenge a friend to a game of chess. Although the game may be viewed as the domain of grandmasters, child geniuses, and computer boffins, the language of chess has infiltrated everyday parlance in a number of ways. So, even if you know little about the game, you can speak the lingo without realizing it. For instance, any game that ends in a draw may be said to have resulted in a *stalemate*, while *check* can refer to any form of control or restraint. *Endgame*, used to describe the final stage of a chess game, can refer figuratively to the denouement of any competitive encounter. The phrase *opening gambit*, from the Italian *gamba* 'leg', refers to an opening move in which a piece is sacrificed to gain some other kind of advantage. Sacrificing a pawn for tactical gain gives rise to the idiom *pawn in the game*, popularized by its use as the title of a song by Bob Dylan. Another word which began life as a chess term is *jeopardy*, from Old French *jeu parti*, meaning a 'divided game'—one which is so even that it is unclear who will win.

Chess

The word *chess* was borrowed from Old French *eschès* (the origin of modern French *échecs*). From this same root comes the word *check*, which refers to a position in which the king is unable to make any legal move; the ultimate origin of both words is the Persian word *shah*, meaning 'king'. When the game was adopted by the Arabs, the phrase *shah mat* 'the king is dead' was coined to refer to the capture of the king; this is the origin of our word *check-mate*. While the names of the pieces used today are mostly of obvious origins, the *rook*—an alternative name for the castle—is more obscure. It has nothing to do with the bird of that name, but instead derives from the Sanskrit word *ratha* 'chariot', the legacy of Indian sets in which this piece was represented by a chariot, or a pair of stylized horses. Another word of Persian origin which is now obsolete is *fers*, from Persian *ferzen* 'wise man', an Old French borrowing used in the Middle Ages to refer to the queen. Also of French origin is the word *pawn*, from Anglo-Norman *paun* 'foot soldier', ultimately derived from Latin *pes* 'foot'. Yet another French borrowing is *stalemate*, referring to a game with no possible winner. In its earliest form, this was known simply as *stale*, from Old French *estale* 'position'; in the eighteenth century *stalemate* was used alongside the alternative *patt*, whose origins lie in an Italian term for a tied vote.

Chess's widespread popularity has led to the coining of phrases from a variety of languages. French idioms such as *en passant* and *en prise* can be used alongside exoticisms like *fianchetto*, the diminutive form of the Italian word *fianco* 'flank', to refer to the movement of a bishop onto a long diagonal. German terms include *Zugzwang*, a compound of *zug* 'move' and *zwang* 'obligation', used of a position when a player is forced to make a move to his disadvantage, and the still more intimidating *Blitz*, or 'lightning', chess— this is also the root of the term used of an intensive military attack (originally *Blitzkrieg* 'lightning war')—especially the air raids on London in 1940. A rich collection of wonderfully abstruse terms describe elaborate chess strategies and formations—the Sicilian defence, Alekhine's gun, the Philidor position—which remain the province of the initiated. One such term which deserves wider recognition is Kotov syndrome; named for the grandmaster Alexander Kotov, this refers to a decision made after long and hard thought but which turns out to be a total disaster. Although we may not know the term, I suspect all of us know the feeling.

Another game of strategy whose origin can be traced back to the Middle Ages, when it was known as *playing at the tables*, is backgammon. The modern name was introduced in the eighteenth century; it derives from the Middle English *gamen* 'game', and is so called because of the way the pieces can be obliged to return to the beginning. As well as backgammon, tables were used for playing *draughts*, whose name describes the act of drawing the pieces diagonally across the board (from a word meaning 'the action of drawing or pulling'). In the USA this game is known as *checkers*, a variant spelling of *chequer*— from Latin *scacarium* 'chess board'. In the fourteenth century it was known by its French name *jeu de dames* ('game of queens')—also the name of a strategy used in chess involving the queen; in Scotland, draughts has been called *dambrod* since the nineteenth century. *Dominoes* takes its name from a French term for a type of winter hood worn by priests, originating in the Latin word *dominus* 'lord'; although the connection remains unclear, it may reflect a similarity in colour.

Also popular since the Middle Ages are various games of chance involving the throw of dice. *Dice*, originally a plural form of the singular *die*, is from the Latin word *datum*, meaning 'something given', in the sense of an outcome that has been determined by fortune. Today, the chancy nature of certain activities may be likened to the roll of a dice—as in the phrase *dicing with death*, and *dicey*. The Turkish word for a dice, *zar*, is the origin of the English word *hazard*, originally the name of a game of chance played with dice for financial stakes. This is the root of *haphazard*, which includes the Old Norse word *happ*, meaning 'luck' or 'fortune'—the source of English *happy*; its earlier meaning is preserved in *hapless* 'unlucky' and the idiom *by happy chance*. The expression *The die is cast*, referring to a decision that has been made and cannot be changed, is a translation of *alea jacta est*—the words attributed to Julius Caesar on crossing the Rubicon, a river in northern Italy, and embarking on a civil war against Pompey and the Senate. This event also gave rise to the expression *crossing the Rubicon*, another phrase referring to the taking of an irrevocable step.

The face carrying the single spot on the dice is known as the *ace*, from Latin *as*, the name of a coin. It was probably the use of this coin as a stake in gambling that led it to be transferred to the name of one side of the dice. Since the ace was the side of the dice with the lowest score, it was also used to signify bad luck and worthlessness. Even worse than rolling an ace was the *ambs-ace*, from Latin *ambas as* 'both ace', where both dice turned up a one. Now obsolete, *ambs-ace* was for a long time an expression signalling misfortune, as in this quotation from Shakespeare's *All's Well That Ends Well*: 'I had rather be in this choice than throw ames-ace for my life.' This use of *ace* was transferred to the equivalent in a pack of cards; although, when *aces are high*, the ace becomes the card with the highest value in the deck. This is the root of idioms such as *to hold all the aces*, describing someone who has the upper-hand in a particular situation, or *to have an ace up one's sleeve*, referring to an advantage that has yet to be made known. This is also the source of the use of *ace* to describe something that is excellent, or someone who excels in a particular field—an appellation that was especially associated with the daring pilots, or *flying aces*, of the First and Second World Wars. It's tempting to imagine that this usage lies behind the use of *ace* to describe an unreturnable serve in tennis; in fact this goes back to the association of *ace* with a single unit—by serving an ace the player has earned a point.

Additional names for the double one are *snake's eyes*, and *crab's eyes*, from which we get the name of the dice game *craps*. A throw of two ones was also known as *deuce*, from the French word for two—the origin of modern French *deux*. Because of the unlucky associations of this roll, which is the lowest score one can achieve with two dice, the word *deuce* came to be associated with bad luck and even with the devil—as in old-fashioned expressions like *What the deuce*. Since the Middle Ages dice have also been known as *bones*, a reference to the material from which they were carved.

Perhaps more stimulating than rolling dice is playing one of the many games making use of packs of playing cards. The word *card* is from Latin *charta* 'papyrus leaf'—also the origin of *charter* and *chart*. We've already seen how the ace was transferred from dice to cards; the origins of the other numerical and royal cards are all straightforward—the exception being the question of what to call the lowest value picture card: *jack* or *knave*? The earlier term is *knave*—from an Old English word meaning 'page, attendant'; *jack*, probably deriving from the widespread use of the personal name *Jack* to refer to any young man, became more common in the nineteenth century. The *OED* suggests that the preference for *jack* over *knave* may have been encouraged by the introduction of letters and numbers on the corners of individual cards; the use of 'j' for *jack* thereby enabled a distinction to be made between the knave and the king. Although it is now the more usual term for the card, *jack* was initially associated with lower-class usage, as is apparent from the scornful way that Estella greets Pip's use of the word in *Great Expectations* (1860–1): 'He calls the knaves, Jacks, this boy!' This use of *jack* is the origin of *jackpot*, which was originally a poker term for the pool of money (or *pot*) that mounted up until one player was able to play two jacks, and thereby begin the bidding.

An important feature of all card games is the ability to *bluff*—the practice of attempting to mislead others into thinking your hand is stronger than it actually is, in the hope that this will prompt them to fold rather than to continue bidding. The word *bluff* is from a Dutch word mean 'brag' or 'boast'; it originally described a blindfold worn by a horse, and then any attempt to hoodwink or trick someone. A player who elects not to fold, but rather to meet his opponent's stake, is said to *call his bluff*—thereby requiring him to reveal the true value of his hand. The idea of bragging probably lies behind the name *poker*, which is thought to originate in the German word *pochen* 'to brag, boast'; it is also preserved in the name of the closely related game *brag*. Ensuring that your opponents are unable to guess the contents of your hand requires the development of a *poker face*: a deadpan expression that conceals your true emotions. This expression also lies behind *po-faced*, which has now acquired the connotations of humourlessness and disapproval.

While bluffing is a legitimate way of attempting to win a game despite being dealt a poor hand, actual cheating is frowned upon. One way of reducing the possibility of players replacing their cards with others was to insist on their hands being visible—above the table. This is where the phrase *above board* originated (*board* being an early word for a table). If your hand is particularly strong, putting you in a commanding position, you are said to *hold all the cards*. But to succeed in this game you must never give away the contents of your hand, or *lay your cards on the table*; instead you should be careful to *keep your cards close to your chest*. If you *play your cards right*, this might just be your lucky night. If things don't go so well, you might find yourself being *given your cards*, that is, getting sacked; this isn't a reference to card games at all—here the cards refer to the documents held by your employer on your behalf and returned when your employment is terminated. If something is likely to happen, it is *on the cards*—a reference to the tarot cards used by fortune tellers to make predictions about the future.

Card games that involve betting usually begin with an *ante*, from Latin 'before', referring to the stake that is put up before the cards are drawn. If another player wishes to raise the stake, he is said to have *upped the ante*—an idiom that is now used more widely to refer to any action that is designed to increase the seriousness of a situation. It is unclear where this use of *stake* originated; one theory is that it derives from the practice of placing an object that was the subject of a wager on a wooden post, but this neat suggestion lacks firm evidence. In a game of poker a marker, known as a *buck*—perhaps because it was the handle of a knife made of buckhorn—was used as a reminder of whose turn it was to deal the cards. When the responsibility to deal was passed to the next player, so was the buck—hence the expression *to pass the buck*. Since the new dealer now took over the responsibility, the related expression *The buck stops here* also emerged. A number of games involve selecting one of the four suits to outrank the other three, known as *trumps*—a variant form of *triumph*. From this we get *trump card*—something that confers a particular advantage—and *turn up trumps*—an eventuality that turns out successfully, deriving from the method of choosing the trump suit by turning over a card.

For a more modern form of entertainment played at the table, you could try a board game. In their simplest manifestation, board games involve moving counters around a board at the throw of a dice. Examples of this kind include Ludo, whose name simply means 'I play' in Latin, and Snakes and Ladders, with the additional twist that counters may climb up ladders or slide down snakes. In other games the counter is replaced by a *meeple*—from a blend of *my* and *people*—where the playing piece is styled to resemble a person. A long-standing family favourite is Monopoly, devised in the USA in the 1930s; *monopoly*, 'exclusive right to supply a commodity or service', is from Greek *mono* 'single' and *polein* 'to sell'. For a test of your general knowledge you could try Trivial Pursuit. While *trivial* now means 'of little significance', it originates in the more serious academic context of the university curriculum of the Middle Ages. The Trivium (from *tri* and *via* 'three ways') was the lower of the two divisions, consisting of grammar, rhetoric, and logic; the upper division was termed the Quadrivium—initially a crossroads, where four roads meet—comprising arithmetic, geometry, astronomy, and music. Together the Trivium and Quadrivium make up the seven liberal arts.

The tabletop football game Subbuteo took its name from the scientific term for the bird of prey *Falco subbuteo* (from *buteo* 'hawk'). The reason behind this apparently strange choice of name is that the game's inventor, Peter Adolph, was not granted a trademark under his preferred name of The Hobby, prompting him to switch instead to the Latin name of the bird of prey known in English as the *hobby*. A similar story is behind the naming of a well-known German car manufacturer founded by German August Horch in the early twentieth century. Discovering that he could not brand his new company Horch, since it was already registered as a trade name, he decided to translate it into Latin; since Horch is the imperative form of the German verb *horchen* 'to listen', the company was named using the imperative form of the Latin verb *audire—Audi*.

Finally, it is time to turn in, go to bed, or ascend *the wooden hill to Bedfordshire*—an expression that is first recorded as early as 1665—perhaps armed with a cup of *cocoa* (an altered form of *cacao*, the seed from which chocolate is made) or *Horlicks*. Named in honour of its manufacturer, William Horlick (1846–1936), it is unfortunate that the brand name is now widely associated with the phrase *make a Horlicks of*, to refer to any disastrous attempt to achieve something, probably originating as a polite alternative to *bollocks*. The *mattress* upon which we lie down, *recline* (Latin *reclinare* 'bend back'), or *recumb* (Latin *recumbere* 'to lie down') comes from the Arabic word *matrah* 'carpet, cushion', or more literally 'place where something is thrown'. *Pillow* is a Germanic word that was originally borrowed from Latin *pulvinus* 'cushion'. Since the Romans were particularly fond of reclining in comfort, they had words for a variety of cushions: *coxinum* 'hip cushion' is the source of English *cushion*. A *bolster* was formerly a soft cushion, but is now more specifically a hard pillow placed underneath a softer one on which the head rests, as well as a verb meaning 'give support to someone or something'. An *eiderdown* gets its name from the fact that it was originally stuffed with the down of the eider—a northern sea bird, whose name is of Old Norse origin. An alternative term, *quilt*, originates in the Latin *culcita*, meaning 'stuffed mattress'. *Duvet* is simply the French word for 'down', adopted into English in the eighteenth century—hence the retention of the French pronunciation. If you've spent the evening over-indulging, tomorrow may turn out to be a *duvet day*—one spent in bed recovering, usually with the tacit approval of one's employer.

Having pulled on your *pyjamas* (from an Urdu word meaning 'leg clothing', referring to loose trousers worn by men and women), or perhaps a *nightdress*, or *negligée*, from a French word meaning 'neglected' or 'given little thought', it's time to go to sleep, or *catch some z's*—an American slang term drawing on the use of 'z' (if pronounced *zee*) to represent the sound of someone snoring. Since 'z' is the last letter in the alphabet it may also be used allusively to represent the end of something—as it is in the idiom *from A to Z*, as is the Greek letter *omega* (literally 'great o', in contrast to *omicron*, or 'little o'). Having travelled from A to Z, or from dawn to dusk, this is a fitting moment to end this day in the life of the English language.

All that remains is to say *goodbye*, a contraction of *God be with ye*, or *Adieu*, from French *à Dieu* 'to God', an abbreviated form of a phrase commending someone to divine protection—a similar origin lies behind the Spanish *Adios*. The Latin *Vale* 'be well' has been used at leave-takings since the sixteenth century; alternatively you might express the wish that someone *fare*, or 'travel', *well*. The many expressions used by and to children include *Da-da*, *TTFN* (*ta-ta for now*), *Shake a day-day*, and *See you later alligator*, with the expected response *In a while crocodile*—popularized by a Bobby Charles song of 1955. If you are feeling pessimistic about the likelihood of a future meeting, you could employ the Japanese *sayonara*, a shortening of *sayo naraba*, 'if it be thus'—similar to the 'if I'm spared' added by gloomy souls to put a dampener on future plans. More upbeat options include *Cheero, Cheerio, Cheery-bye*—drawing upon the much earlier greeting *What cheer?* The 1920s gave us several more or less ludicrous formations based on the verb *toot*—*Toodle-oo, Toodle-pip, Pip-pip*—perfectly acceptable if you want to sound like Bertie Wooster exiting the Drones Club, but riskier in other social situations. In an attempt to appear more sophisticated you might turn to the Italian

Ciao—which may be used when greeting or parting—though be careful who you say it to, since it literally means 'I am your slave' (from Latin *sclavus* 'slave'). Perhaps more appropriate for this particular farewell is an alternative Italian salutation, *Arrivederci*, meaning 'until we see each other again'—used to express affectionate good wishes in the expectation and desire of meeting again at some point in the future.

Further Reading

This book draws heavily upon a number of key scholarly resources for the study of etymology. Most valuable have been the detailed and *egregious*—and here I'm using the word in its earliest sense of 'excellent' (literally 'standing out from the flock')—etymologies supplied by the *Oxford English Dictionary*, which are the starting point for anyone interested in researching the histories of English words. I have drawn extensively upon these throughout this book, supplementing and cross-referencing them with various other etymological dictionaries cited below. Another resource that I have plundered shamelessly is the *Historical Thesaurus of the OED,* which organizes the *OED* entries according to their meanings. *Thesaurus* is from a Greek word meaning 'storehouse'; it was initially used of dictionaries and encyclopedias—the current sense was established following the publication of a *Thesaurus of English Words and Phrases* (1852) by the physician Peter Mark Roget, whose name is now synonymous with this book of synonyms. The Greek word *thesaurus* is also the origin of English *treasure*, a word that better captures the value of the *eximious*, *prestantious*, and *supernacular Historical Thesaurus of the OED.*

Oxford English Dictionary, 3rd edition (in progress), www.oed.com

Historical Thesaurus of the Oxford English Dictionary, ed. C. Kay et al. (Oxford: Oxford University Press, 2009); available online at https://ht.ac.uk

Barnhart, Robert K. (ed.), *Chambers Dictionary of Etymology* (Edinburgh: Chambers, 1999).

Crystal, David, *Words in Time and Place: Exploring Language through the Historical Thesaurus of the Oxford English Dictionary* (Oxford: Oxford University Press, 2014).

Crystal, David, *Words, Words, Words* (Oxford: Oxford University Press, 2006).

Durkin, Philip, *Borrowed Words: A History of Loanwords in English* (Oxford: Oxford University Press, 2014).

Durkin, Philip, *The Oxford Guide to Etymology* (Oxford: Oxford University Press, 2009).

Gilliver, Peter, *The Making of the Oxford English Dictionary* (Oxford: Oxford University Press, 2016).

Hitchings, Henry, *The Secret Life of Words: How English Became English* (London: John Murray, 2008).

Horobin, Simon, *The English Language: A Very Short Introduction* (Oxford: Oxford University Press, 2018).

Hughes, Geoffrey, *A History of English Words* (Oxford: Blackwell, 2000).

Hughes, Geoffrey, *Words in Time: A Social History of English Vocabulary* (Oxford: Blackwell, 1988).

Jones, Peter, *Quid Pro Quo: What the Romans Really Gave the English Language* (London: Atlantic Books, 2016).

Liberman, Anatoly, *Word Origins...and How We Know Them* (Oxford: Oxford University Press, 2009).

Onions, C. T., G. W. S. Friedrichsen, and R. W. Burchfield (eds.), *The Oxford Dictionary of Etymology* (Oxford: Clarendon Press, 1966).

Simpson, John, *The Word Detective. A Life in Words: From Serendipity to Selfie* (London: Little, Brown, 2016).

Index of Words

H

Index of People